A FLIGHT AND A FERRARI

notionpress.com

A FLIGHT AND A FERRARI

KARUPPAN

notionpress.com

Notion Press

Old No. 38, New No. 6

McNichols Road, Chetpet

Chennai - 600 031

First Published by Notion Press 2016

ISBN 978-93-5206-851-7

Table of Contents

1

Destiny Rings in the New Year

December 31, 2003. It's New Year's Eve, and a typical nippy *margazhi* winter evening in Chennai.

The four of us – Nutty, Srinath, Deepan and I - all in our teens or early twenties, are excited about the New Year and we are eagerly discussing various options on how to celebrate. Simbu, the fifth member of what Enid Blyton would have called the "Friendly Five" group, is in London to shoot for a film. Simbu is my cousin and since childhood, we have always been very close to one another. I am also the favourite nephew to his parents. I miss Simbu a lot today and I know the celebrations would not be complete without him. My friends miss him too and we are already trying to think of ways to involve him in the celebrations.

"Hey, why not start the celebrations by visiting Simbu's house, spending some time with aunty and uncle and wishing them a happy New Year...?" suggests Nutty. Good idea! Off we go to Simbu's house.

As we drive down to Simbu's house, probably for the first time in my life, I start thinking about what the New Year holds for me, about what the future holds for me. I realize that I am on the threshold of a very important phase of my life and I ought to be seriously planning my future course of action. Something tells me that 2004 is going to be a very important and decisive year in my life. Strangely, I also feel that my life is going to be a struggle but at the end of it all, I will emerge a winner.

As I start reviewing my life this far, I begin to feel happy and proud that I was always a good student. My memories go back to the years I spent as a student at Santhome Higher Secondary School and I also distinctly remember the day when I got a hundred in maths in the 10th standard exams. I had promised Mom that I would get a centum and I had done it. Oh, what a day it was! I felt on top of the world and it also gave me a tremendous amount of confidence at that point in life.

After school, I had chosen to do Production Engineering and for me, clearing semesters did not prove to be difficult... I was not a bookworm but thanks to my power of observation and assimilation, I was able to do well and stay ahead of others in the class. And yes, while at college, I took to modelling and also participated in intercollege cultural competitions where my talents in logo designing and art came to the fore. It was probably because of this that my parents had been convinced and hopeful that I would take up acting as a profession...but I was not keen to enter films in spite of the fact that I attended Shanthi master's class for two years and also grew up in the company of predictably big stars of the future.

As the flashback continued, I realised that I had always wanted to be different. I had never felt comfortable doing things the routine way. Going that extra mile, swimming against the tide, exploring new territory and wanting to excel in anything I did seemed to be my natural trait. But how was this realisation going to help me choose my career? What did the future hold? And what part would destiny play? I really did not know.

The car enters Simbu's residence. It's 8 p.m. We enter the house and wish uncle and aunty a very happy New Year.

We get down to talking about how Simbu's shooting is progressing in London and about how we all miss him on this very auspicious day. I have always treated uncle as a good friend too: I tell him about my concern about the future. With a strong accent and almost like prophesying, he replies "You have always worked hard and I am sure you will have a great future... yes, like everybody, you too could face a lot of struggles in life but believe me, you'll emerge a winner. Go with the flow, work hard, allow destiny to shape your future and have faith in God." We continue talking for a while; the New Year is the subject of our discussion and I also tell him how much I miss Simbu today.

It's 8.30 p.m. and my mobile phone starts ringing... think of the devil and..., my God, it's Simbu! I answer the call and his first words are, "*Ennada eppidi irruke*? (Hi, how are you?)... it's very lonely down here in London... can you take a flight and join me so that we can spend the New Year here?" "Even if you take a late night flight today or an early morning flight tomorrow, you can still reach London in time to celebrate New Year..." Without a second thought, I say, "OK *da*, book my tickets but do me a favour... make it a Chennai-London-San Jose circuit ticket as I would like to spend a couple of days in the US before I return home." "Done," he says.

The first thing I do is call home and inform mom about my trip to London and the US. I can sense Mom's concern by the way she speaks but at the end of the conversation she says, "Okay, go ahead, but once you're in London and then the US, it will be up to you to take care of yourself... you must learn to stand on your own feet and I would not like you to depend on us for any financial help... anyway, since it's only for a few days, I'm sure you can manage... good luck son!." "Thanks Mom," I say and she disconnects.

Mom has always been a tremendous source of support to me. Right from the time I can remember, she's always been there for me. There are times when I have gone up to her and cried over trivial issues which I could not handle as a child. Even as an adult, there are occasions when I have gone to her with tears in my eyes and like magic, her words of comfort have made the tears disappear. I have never kept anything from her and I never will. Another thing I know is that as a mom, she has tremendous confidence in me and is convinced that I will make a mark in life.

Whenever I think of Mom, a true story I read about Thomas Edison comes to my mind and I would like to share this story here. While at school, Edison was once rebuked by his teacher who told him that he was an "addled" (unable to think clearly, confused) child. When he told his mother about this, she stormed into the teacher's room and declared, "My son's not backward" and when the teacher refused to change her opinion about Edison, his mother is believed to have said, "All right, I am hereby taking my son out of your school... I'll instruct him at home myself." Tom was astounded by his mother's trust and confidence in him and he promised himself that he would make his mother proud of him. Later in life, Edison is believed to have said "My mother was the making of me. She was so true, so sure of me; and I felt I had something to live for, someone I must not disappoint."

Today, on New Year's Eve, I too promise myself that I would work hard to make a mark in life and would do my mother proud. I will not disappoint her. I will not let her down on the trust and confidence she has in me. It's a New Year resolution and I am determined that this is one resolution I will not break. Promise!

My Chennai-London-San Jose tickets are booked and as per the itinerary, my Chennai-London British Airways flight is scheduled to take off early morning tomorrow and my London-San Jose flight has been booked for 6th January. Simbu has confirmed that he will be waiting at the airport to receive me.

It's past midnight and the New Year has arrived. I am happy that I will be celebrating New Year twice, once in Chennai and then, again in London. The celebrations have begun and as I take part, my thoughts are divided between Chennai and London. I go home and pack my things in just one bag because I decide to travel light and more so, because I would be staying abroad for just about a fortnight.

It suddenly strikes me that for the first time in my life, I will be travelling alone and that too, to a foreign country. Even on domestic flights, I have always travelled with my mother or brother or someone else in the family. Yes, this is going to be a new experience for me and I am already feeling confident of facing up to any new challenges that destiny has in store for me.

I bid goodbye to Mom and all my loved ones at home. As I prepare to leave, my Mom says, "Remember, you are on your own from now on and until you are back... enjoy yourself but do not fail to notice the opportunities that come your way. My blessings are with you... do call me up whenever you feel like speaking with me..."

I get into the car and head towards the airport. As the day's events unfold and I think about my uncle's advice and my mom's words, something tells me that the journey I am about to undertake is going to be a potential game changer that would influence my future to a great extent.

2

London, Here I Come...

At Chennai International Airport, I decide to check in my only baggage so that I can have a hands-free, comfortable journey. I am booked as an Economy class passenger and after receiving the boarding pass, proceed for immigration, security, and other formalities. By about 3 a.m., I am ready to board the British Airways early morning flight. The flying time from Chennai to London is about eleven hours and I am aware that we are five hours ahead of London time. This means, I will be landing in London at about 10 a.m. local time today, the first of January 2004.

Boarding is announced and in the next couple of minutes, I am settling down in my window seat. I am excited about travelling to London and that too alone... I am excited about celebrating the New Year again in a different country. Above all, I am excited that Simbu and I are going to enjoy ourselves during my stay there. The aircraft is ready for take-off, and as it begins to move forward, I enjoy the thrill of the momentum as well as the feel of the aircraft leaving the ground and soaring towards the skies. The experience has always fascinated me, maybe, because it reminds me of my bike racing days. London, here I come!

As I sink further into my seat, my ticket book (three or four leaves of thin paper bound together and resembling a mini cheque book) sticks out of my pocket and lest it falls out when I am asleep, I put it inside the pouch in front of my seat. I notice that the pouch also holds the in-flight magazine as well as other safety literature and my tickets are safely entrenched in between. I make sure that my passport is in my pocket and there is no way it can slip out.

Comfortably settled, I reset my watch to London time and decide to sleep but am too excited to fall asleep immediately. I think about mom and her words about a career in the US. I also think about the promise I made to myself about making her proud, and am somehow convinced that this is going to be more than a pleasure trip. I have this feeling that I am cruising in the right direction and with this thought, fall asleep.

Six hours into the flight, I wake up. It's bright outside, but most of the passengers are still sleeping. I go to sleep again only to be woken up by the in-flight staff serving breakfast. We still have about two hours to go. After breakfast, I browse through some of the magazines and when the pilot announces that we are going to land, the excitement builds up in me. I look around and notice that only a few children in the front row look as excited as me.

The aircraft lands spot-on time in Heathrow airport and as it comes to a halt and we are allowed to get off, I am up from my seat making my way to the exit. Hands free, I head towards the Customs and Immigration desk and as I walk down, I am amazed at the cleanliness and the ambience of the airport. A pleasant 20 something blond female with a smile on her face, asks me to produce my tickets and passport... I delve into my pockets... cannot find the tickets... frantically check my shirt insides...oh my God! In my excitement, I seem to have forgotten to take the tickets from the pouch in front of my seat on the plane! I reach for my mobile to try and call Simbu but realize that I am not carrying one.

I curse myself. Mixed emotions of guilt, helplessness, and a "how-could-I-have-forgotten" feeling envelopes me and with an "I'm-so-sorry" sheepish look on my face, explain my position to the staff. "Ok, let's check out the passenger list from the airline crew...do you remember the seat number?" "Yes, I do, it was A60." She puts her nimble fingers into action and calls up her immediate superior, explains the scene to him and requests him to arrange for a copy of the passenger list of my flight. One by one, the passengers behind me complete the formalities and make their way to the exit. After what seems to be like an eternity, the list is verified and when they are convinced that I am a genuine passenger, let me go after issuing an immigration clearance certificate on a duplicate set of tickets. As I am leaving, she says "Welcome to London, have a great stay." My feelings of guilt vanish. I had just learnt two lessons – lesson number one, always keep your travel documents on your person and lesson number two, it makes sense to take copies of all the documents and keep them separately.

I pick up my bag and look out for Simbu but am not able to spot him anywhere. I walk down slowly towards the exit and as I do so, continue to try and see if Simbu is somewhere in the crowd. I am again awed by the beauty of the airport and see people of different nationalities... new faces, a totally new atmosphere... and excitement builds up again. I feel a gentle pat on my shoulder... it's Simbu with his usual "Hai *da*...Happy New Year!" We hug each other and soon, are on our way to the city. Yes, I am in the city of London and what a thrill to be here!

We take a tube from the airport to reach the London YMCA where Simbu is staying. This is the first time I am travelling by the tube and I am greatly impressed with the clockwork precision of the operations as well as the plush interiors of the coaches. As we pass through brightly lit stations, I eagerly look forward to reaching our destination. In about twenty minutes, we are at the YMCA Hostel. The 5' x 10' room, in which Simbu has been staying has a bunker cot, and this is going to be my home, sweet home for the next few days.

We freshen up and Simbu says "Let's go around the city and see how we can celebrate the New Year." We are joined by another friend, Isaac, and together, begin to explore the city. We are hungry, and our first stop is Starbucks where I settle for some bagels and a cup of Cappuccino. As I sip my coffee, I become conscious of the fact that this capital city has a lot to offer in terms of life time experiences that could interest as well as intrigue and I am eager to explore

From Starbucks, we again take a tube and our next stop is the Tower of London on the banks of River Thames in central London. What an astounding piece of architecture! I just cannot believe that this place was used as a prison during the First and Second World Wars and that it had also seen twelve people being executed for espionage. Over the next few days, we also visit the Buckingham Palace, London Bridge, the Madam Tussauds Wax Museum, and many more interesting places. Piccadilly Circus (circus is Latin for "circle") specially attracts me because of its proximity to the shopping and entertainment spots and also for its fabulous video displays and neon signs. We also visit some of the renowned pubs to get a feel of the place and do a bit of dancing.

We are scheduled to leave London tomorrow, that is, the 6th of January and I tell Simbu that we must visit a Casino before we go. "We'll do it today," he says. It is about 8 p.m. and we enter the Hippodrome Casino in Leicester Square.

Three gaming floors, an underground casino, a 180-seat music and cabaret room, six bars, a steak house... oh my God!, What a feel!... just like straight out of the English westerns! We walk around the casino tables – we learn that there are 45 traditional tables – and for the first time in my life I get to see the Roulette, Blackjack, Three Card Poker, Dice, Pai Gow, Baccarat, and the Casino War tables. People are all over, trying their luck. Currency (Pounds) is thrown in, tables swirl around and the winner takes it all! I look around and some of them look back at me possibly wondering if I am trying to influence the game. Phew! After about two hours and a light dinner at the 24-hour Steak House restaurant, we are back in the YMCA for tomorrow's flight – Simbu flies to Chennai and I fly to San Jose.

Simbu suggests we go to bed early since we have to take the early morning flights, and we set the alarm accordingly. Simbu's flight is five hours ahead of mine, and we decide that both of us will leave for the airport together and after seeing him off, I would spend some time looking around, in the airport. I call up a good friend, James, in San Jose and tell him that I am coming over and would be staying with him for a couple of days. Way back, my Mom had helped James's parents organise and celebrate their 60th wedding anniversary in Chennai and probably, he had not forgotten this good deed. "Great, come over... I'll get my brother, Kerry to pick you up at the airport," says James.

The clock ticks on but I don't get sleep. There is a sense of regret that my stay in London is coming to an end, and equally, there is also a feel of suspense as to how the US is going to be for me. Thoughts keep flashing by... how long will

I stay in the US.... what am I going for... is the fun phase over with London and is it going to be tough in the US....? I get back to thinking of Mom, the promise I made to myself and once again, I am determined to make a mark in life: I fall asleep.

3

The Land of Opportunity Beckons

It's January 6th and I am booked Economy class on the United Airlines afternoon flight to San Jose. I need to change planes at Chicago and the total flying time would be about fourteen hours. Just before we leave for the airport, I realize that I don't have any money with me, and just about then, as if he was reading my mind, Simbu asks me if I have any money with me. I reply in the negative and he immediately takes out a hundred-dollar note and hands it over to me saying "Keep this, you'll need it..." I admire him for his thoughtfulness and at the same time, am pleasantly surprised as to how my needs are being fulfilled without even asking, and wonder if this is an indication of how things will be for me in the New Year.

Simbu and I leave the YMCA together and at the airport, he suggests that I too go inside. We enter the airport, bid goodbye... he proceeds to complete the formalities. I walk down to check out on my flight which is scheduled to depart about five hours later. A few steps ahead, a ticketing staff from the airline waves me over... "Are you flying to Chicago?" he asks. I nod and after he sees my ticket, tells me, "There's a flight leaving in the next one hour and if you're okay to take the flight, we can upgrade you to Business class." Well, why would I not agree? Apart from saving a couple of hours, I would also be travelling Business class for the first time in my life. When I agree, since there is very little time left, the airline staff escorts me all the way up to the check-in counter, bypassing the queue at different points. Wow! I've only seen VIPs enjoy such privileges, and I already feel the positive vibrations around me.

It's just unbelievable and as I check-in and get ready for boarding, I wonder if destiny has begun her courtship with me... otherwise, how could I have arrived at the airport early, how did Simbu tell me to go inside the airport rather than stay outside, how could the airline personnel have identified me in particular?... how could?... well, the questions are many, and I have no answers. I feel very happy and the orthodox Hindu that I am, believe that sentimentally this is a good beginning.

I board the aircraft and occupy my seat. An hour into the flight, I decide to push back my seat but don't know how to do it... remember, I am flying business class first time. Embarrassed, I look around, watch the girl next to me push her seat back, take her cue, and manage to do it. We land at O'Hare International airport in Chicago on time and after getting immigration cleared, as I walk down to take my connecting flight to San Jose, I am awed by the size of the airport, the beauty of snow falling, and begin to wonder as to how flights manage to take off or land in such weather. O'Hare, incidentally, is the busiest airport in the world by the number of take offs and landings and also the sixth busiest by passenger traffic.

As the aircraft begins its descent to land in San Jose, the view is fantastic and the weather seems to be just right. Kerry, receives me at the airport, and after a twenty minute drive, we reach the four-bedroom house located in the town of Milpitas. There are a total of five people staying in the house, and each room is shared by two people. I share my room with Kerry. I am tired and decide to stay indoors for the rest of the day.

During the next few days, my friends show me around – malls, California Theatre, Municipal Rose Garden, Stevens Creek, Happy to Hollow Park and Zoo and lot more.

It's raining lightly. The rains are invigorating and a pleasure to experience, but also create a feel of vacuum... a sense of loneliness. If you've ever been alone at home, away from your loved ones on a rainy winter night, you'll know what I mean. Ever since I land in San Jose, at the end of each day, as the sound of battering rain keeps on, I feel lonely and since loneliness always leads to a longing for your loved ones, I remember Mom... I miss her. How nice it would be if she too was here... and yes, whenever I think of Mom, I remember my promise too.

Five days have passed since I landed and it's 12th January. After breakfast (all meals are cooked at home by my roommates), I walk down to the gas station close by, randomly pick up a newspaper, and notice an ad by a company calling for sales personnel. The name of the company is Brunocorp and they are involved in helping residents who are shifting, move their belongings. I call and am asked to come over and meet Gidon, the boss, tomorrow.

Thirteenth January 10 a.m. Dekel, the receptionist at Brunocorp, receives me and after a few minutes, I meet Gidon in his cabin. "Where are you from?" he asks me. "India," I reply and with a smile on his face asks me, "Okay, but where in India?" When I tell him that I'm from Chennai, he tells me that his wife Shula has been to Chennai and that she also rode pillion on a Bullet. I give him a small brief about myself and also tell him that if recruited, I would ensure that the company's profits soar. His immediate reaction is, "You seem to have a very thick accent but you also seem to have the determination to succeed and the confidence to perform... I think I'll give you an opportunity... you are hired." My salary is a little over one hundred and fifty dollars per week plus commission.

Soon, Gidon's wife, Shula joins us and at this point his face turns pale and he says, "You know something, my pet dog Frono died this morning..." and he is unable to go on. Gidon and his wife get emotional and the tears in their eyes tell me, more than words can express, as to how much they loved Frono. Since I too have a dog back home in Chennai, I understand how they feel and I suppress the tears welling up in my eyes. RIP Frono. Gidon is in mourning and does not turn up at the office for a week.

At my new job, I am introduced to Nadav, an Ethiopian national, who would, in the next few days, provide me with an orientation of the systems and procedures adopted at Brunocorp. My responsibilities are to speak with potential customers, tell them about services offered, and costing involved, convince them and then close the deal.

Nadav informs me that the Company undertakes intra state moves. He also goes on to tell me that since the volumes are very low, everyone is under pressure to perform, and that in spite of the team's best efforts, business does not seem to be coming in. He also gives me an indication of the number of calls being made as well as the sales figures during the previous financial year, both of which are pathetically low. I empathize with him but at the same time, also like what he is telling me because I now know that I can look forward to challenges, and will have an opportunity to face up to such challenges and prove myself.

After my first day in the office, I reach my room and inform Kerry and the others about my new job. Kerry is okay, but the others speak discouragingly and try to dissuade me. I tell them that I am determined to go ahead, and I also offer to pay them rent for my stay. Since I do not know to cook and everyone is supposed to share the chores, I tell them that I will do the washing up of the utensils used for cooking while they will continue to do the cooking. I also tell them, "I will review the scene after about three months and if I feel like continuing on the job, I'll move out and find another place to stay." They agree.

I call home and speak to Mom and tell her about landing a job. She is happy for me and all she says is "My blessings are with you... keep going as long as you can, but anytime you want to quit and come back, we're there for you...."

Day two in the office. Nadav shows me the rate card for services offered by the company... it's got the services listed in the first section and the corresponding charges are listed in the rear section. It's just like the log book I had while doing my Engineering, and as such, I am able to assimilate the details with ease. On the whole, I feel that the job is going to be a cakewalk; the more I think about it, the more confident I feel. Destiny's courtship continues, I presume.

The distance between my place of stay and my office is about three kilometres. On the first day, I get dropped at office by one of my roommates and in the evening, walk back home. On the second day, I walk down to the office and in the evening, again walk back home. It's raining very heavily and quite dark too. I do not remember having witnessed such heavy rains even during the winter season anywhere in India. It's also very cold and I'm shivering... it seems to be the longest walk I have ever had. After I reach home and dry myself, I call up Mom and tell her about my condition and she says "Don't worry, we're here... just don't give up and everything will be okay."

The next day, I borrow Gidon's cycle. The second day I use the cycle, it is again raining heavily and pitch dark. Just minutes after I leave the office, the cycle hits against something hard... thud... and oops!, I am thrown off! I manage to get up, brace myself, and check for injuries... just a couple of scratches. Fully drenched, I pick up the cycle, straighten out the handlebar, and start pushing it towards my room. As the rain drops fall on my bare skin, I feel a burning sensation due to the scratches... but more painful, is the ache in my heart due to being emotionally upset over this unfortunate incident. I slowly trudge along... the burning sensation is getting better, but the heartache is getting worse...

I don't tell any of my friends about the incident that night, but when everyone's asleep, I tiptoe down to the backyard, look at the cycle, and start weeping! I don't tell Mom. I remember what my uncle told me on New Year's Eve.

4

An Action Plan that Succeeds

The next day, I decide to try out a different mode of transportation... something adventurous, something unique. I have my first week's pay, and I choose to buy a motorized skate scooter costing 110 dollars. It runs on petrol, and has an entrenched metal sling which one needs to pull up to start the vehicle... just like what they use in some of the generators in India. It makes a lot of noise and can get people to stare at you, but I don't mind.

As I return from office on my skate scooter on the second day of usage, it continues to rain heavily, and it is also very dark. Believe it or not, I do a repeat performance... the skate scooter skids, and I crash against a wall and am thrown off. "Oh no, not again," I tell myself. This time, the heartache comes back, and as I retrieve the skate scooter and start pushing it home, I get into depression mode again. The emotional feel is heavier this time. Again, I don't tell Mom.

At office, as days pass by, I am beginning to understand my job better. I tell myself that I must get to become the best performer in the office, and for this, I first need to check out on how the other sales personnel are performing. About fifty calls per day seem to be the norm, and the company has just a little over twenty orders on hand, at this point of time. Over the past few days I too have been trying to make as many calls as possible but the maximum number on an average per day has been just about forty. The response too has not been very encouraging, and conversions just do not seem to be happening. So, what do I do...?

I first decide to identify the causes for not being able to perform well. I also decide that as I get to identify the causes, I will also simultaneously try and find ways by which the negatives can be eliminated. As I set about my task and start thinking deeply, I am pleasantly surprised to find that I am not only able to pinpoint the negatives with ease but at the same time, am also able to identify ways to correct myself. I key in my plan of action on the computer and something tells me that like at the London airport, this time too destiny will play her role and all is going to be well. With a determination like never before, I decide to put my plan into action...

First, the way I speak. Some of the customers, whom I had called, had been blunt in saying, "You have a very thick accent." I also remember one of the customers yelling at me and telling me "Get lost, you Indian." In fact, I must also admit that as a newcomer, I had not even been aware that the "J" in San Jose is silent and had been pronouncing the name wrongly all the time. I'm sure many customers were lost because of the way I spoke.

So, how do I get this right? I remember having read somewhere that if accent or modulation needs to be improved, one has to practise outdoors early in the morning. So, I write down my sales pitch, go outdoors every morning, and with fog and drizzle keeping me company, I read out the script loudly over and over again, maybe a hundred times. At the office, I start making more number of phone calls, not in the hope of increasing the conversions, but because I want to talk more, test out my accent with customers, and also listen to how they speak so that I can emulate. After a couple of days, I know my accent is getting better when I hear the way my customers respond to my sales pitch and also when I notice that they are paying serious attention to everything that I say.

Next on my plan of action, is to watch and learn. I decide to observe my colleagues and get to pick up the key words they use while speaking to customers. I, then, include these words in my sales pitch too.

Observe and act, is the third on my list. I had always observed Shula speaking to customers on the phone, and I was amazed that almost every call she made, she was successful in clinching the deal. And, I knew it was much more than because she was a lady. Ever since I joined Brunocorp, she had been doing everything she could to encourage me to perform well. So now, whenever I am free, I walk down to her cubicle and keenly watch how she does her sales pitch... the words she use, her modulation, and so on. I notice that she is always to the point and does not beat around the bush. More than being persuasive, the way she communicates, I thought, clearly impressed the customer. It was difficult to emulate her, but I did try and succeed to a great extent. I knew that with time, I would improve.

Have a heart-to-heart chat with Gidon, is next on my list. On a Monday morning, I walk into his cabin and going to the point directly, say, "Chief, I know I am not doing as well as I intend to do... I just want to tell you that I am trying seriously, and trust me, I will certainly deliver as promised..." He gets up from his seat, comes over, and putting his arm around my shoulder, says, "Yes, I know... I also know that you are very persistent, and you don't give up easily... if you're persistent, you'll be successful... I trust you, have faith in you, and I know you'll do well." What a sweet guy, I think.

Gidon then goes on to tell me a beautiful story that I will never forget in my life. He says, "Imagine a pond with small fishes in it and only one small hole... if the fishes want to go out of the pond, they can only do so one by one. The situation is the same in our business now because in the winter, very few people move house... we're now in the winter. Now, imagine that over a period of time, the hole in the pond gets bigger and bigger... what will happen? Obviously, a school of fish will rush out... now, this is like the spring season when a lot of families will decide to shift and, this is the time, we need to make a kill... so, be patient and prepare for the kill." I realize that he is right and thank him for his advice and the confidence he reposed in me.

Make Mom too a part of my action plan, is the last point on my list. I think of Mom and want her to somehow be a part of my action plan but am not sure as to how I can do it. Then, suddenly I remember having read somewhere about how passwords can help motivate, and so this is what I do. On my computer, I change my password to read as "*promise4mom*" so that every time I sat on the computer, I would be reminded about the promise I made to myself about doing my Mom proud. I find this very satisfying.

"What next?" I ask myself. Curiosity and thirst for knowledge have always been my strengths and at Brunocorp, I am now keen to know more about how other departments work. I also believe that if I get to know the company better, my sales pitch too would be much more effective. I have always had a craze for cars, race bikes and even trucks, and so, my first choice is the transportation department. During lunch breaks, I walk down to have a look at the trucks. I get friendly with the drivers and they explain the operating systems of the vehicles.

For the first time I see that handbrakes actually work and are used by drivers in these trucks. Back home in India, how many of us know that handbrakes are non-existent in trucks, and bricks placed in front and back of the wheels do the job? As I admire the aerodynamics of the vehicles, I also notice the vast expanse of bare and plain side panels of the truck and it strikes me a bit odd. To me, they look like unpainted vinyl hoarding sites... wait a minute... yes, I got it... I have an idea... damn it, the space needs to be used to our benefit!!!

I rush into Gidon's cabin and tell him, "Gidon, I've got an idea... why not create a visual design that carries our company's logo and also conveys what business we're in and get it painted on the side panels of all our trucks...?" Gidon is unable to visualise the design or understand the benefits, but when I explain to him and also tell him that I have won competitions in logo designing and would be happy to work on the design during my spare time, I can see his face brighten up and he says, "What a brainwave... go ahead."

I work on the design, and freeze on the option I like the best. I show this to Gidon, and both he and Shula are highly impressed with the design, and the trucks get a new look... and yes, we also get enquiries from those who have seen the design on the trucks while travelling on the highway. Gidon and his wife are mighty pleased, and their love and affection for me increases. Now, I am almost treated like one in the family, and I too am happy for Gidon and his wife.

5

The Dark Side… Learning it the Hard Way

I am into my second month at Brunocorp, and I can see that my action plan is giving results, and I am getting better and better on my job. At any given point of time, I have 600 leads and on an average, I call 225 customers in a day. My accent is much better, I speak with confidence, and my conversion rate soars. For the first time in the history of Brunocorp, between Nadav and me, we touch eighty orders per month. Gidon and his wife are pleased, and I promise them that this is just the beginning. It is now, that Gidon decides to downsize sales personnel... Nadav and I stay on, and the other sales personnel are asked to leave.

Back in my room too, I can feel the increased flow of positive vibes from Kerry and my other friends and it is obvious that they are pleased with the way things are working out in my favour. I tell myself that I too must take all efforts to reciprocate and strengthen the bond of friendship, and this I should do in such a way that they feel they have a true friend in me. I wonder how I can do this.

It's Friday and I am back home early in the evening. I know my friends will not be back till 6.30, and as I start thinking about what I can do to make them happy, I get an idea. Why not surprise them by cooking dinner? I've never ever cut a potato or even sliced an onion in my life... but the urge to try out something new, to experiment and to do something that I have never done in my life, gets my adrenalin pumping, and I am eager to start... I don't know but maybe, I am also trying to test myself to check if I can be successful in everything I do... I decide to get down to action.

I pick up the phone, call up Mom and ask her to give me instructions on how to prepare chicken curry. She is both surprised and amused. She first lists out the ingredients and asks me to call her back after I am ready. In about twenty minutes, I am all set and call Mom again. I switch on the speaker phone and as she explains, step by step... I follow her instructions... the aroma starts building up and my God! I just cannot believe it... for the first time in my life, I really seem to be enjoying cooking! In minutes, delicious, mouth-watering Chettinad Chicken Curry is ready.

My friends are back and I tell them that today, it's going to be Chettinad Chicken Curry for dinner. They presume that I have ordered food from outside but when they get to know that I have cooked for them, they are surprised and don't believe me. As they start eating, I can see that they are really pleased and the look on their faces makes me happy that I've made them feel good and yes, the dish is tasty too! After dinner, and a couple of burps, one of them remarks "And all the while, you were hiding the fact that you are a great cook eh?" How do I convince them that this is the first time? They just refuse to believe that this is my debut in cooking.

My circle of friends keeps increasing thanks to my participation in cricket matches, birthday and other parties as well as by my occasional visits to restaurants and pubs. I am also beginning to notice that destiny is continuing her courtship with me because, wherever I go and whatever I do, things seem to be just falling in place and working out in my favour without much of an effort on my part. Everyone tends to believe that I am a great performer in whatever I do.

Here's an incident that demonstrates what I mean. Like most youngsters, I too have played cricket in school and college and must admit that I am just an average cricketer. On a Saturday morning, as my friends meet up to play a league cricket match, I agree to be part of the team, and they ask me what I can do. Without a second thought I reply, "I can bowl medium pace and I can also bat," and the next thing I know, they ask me to open the bowling. As I run down the pitch, I find the ball slipping out of my hand but manage to deliver what I know is a bad ball. As luck would have it, the batsman, Sajid, gloves the ball and is given out. Everyone thinks I am a great player but again, I know it's destiny that is playing up to me.

Ever since I landed in San Jose, many a time, as I have looked around, I have noticed that there are hardly any similarities between India and the US. Everything seems to be so different here and today, India seems to appear foreign to me. However, this perception is short-lived as I learn the hard way, that similarities between the two countries do exist but unfortunately, only where it relates to crime, cheating, mistrust and other negative factors. Here's how I got to experience this...

Commuting to and from the office continues to be a problem and since I am now earning a decent salary and can afford it, decide to buy a car. I check out a popular website and after looking at the used car listings, zero in on a beige colour 1985 Ford Escort hatchback. When I ask Nadav to come with me to take delivery of the car, he agrees but even though all his papers are in order, warns me that we could get pulled up by the cops. I don't understand but I am sure Nadav has a reason to fear.

As we drive down and as we are nearing our destination, just as Nadav had predicted, we hear the siren and two cops catch up with us and wave us to stop. I ask the cops what it's all about and they say, "You guys better get out of the car as we need to search." Nadav starts fuming and begins to argue with the cops but I plead to him and ask him to stay cool so that we get over this without any incident.

Nadav and I are asked to place our outstretched hands on the bonnet and the cops frisk us. It just takes a couple of minutes and when they are done, we are allowed to go. Once, we resume our drive, Nadav goes on to explain that blacks in the US are prone to such treatment and it is nothing but racism. I remember the time when I too got pulled up by the cops back home in Chennai and I had to pay up without any argument... it was not racism, though.

We go and take delivery of the 1985 Ford Escort for 250 dollars, and it's a great relief as I no longer need to depend on anyone for transport. I also feel a sense of pride and achievement on owning my first car in the US. Mom is happy too and she says "You're on the right track... keep going... you still have a long way to go..."

The second incident happens on a Friday when Nadav invites me to a party at his place in downtown San Jose. There is music and dance, and as I am enjoying myself, I feel someone tap me on the back, and the next thing I know, I am pushed and fall on the floor, face down. I say a small prayer. My sides hurt as people rush by me, their shoes grazing my body. People seem to be walking over me! After a few minutes, I manage to get up and see a couple of men rushing out of the room, and as I check for injury, find just a few bruises on my face and lips. I sit down on the couch and out of intuition, feel for my wallet but it's not there... it's lying on the floor. I pick it up, and find all the money gone! Later in the night, I remember how a good friend of mine had his pocket picked while travelling on a bus in Chennai. Yes indeed, similarities did exist between India and the US.

Now, here's the shocker! Since my main objective while at work was to learn, gain more experience, get to know the moving business better, and also help Gidon increase revenue, I did not realise that I was missing out on something very very important to me... I noticed that the amount of money being paid to me as wages did not tally with the amount that was actually due to me! I was getting much lesser than what was promised! While I was told that my weekly wages would be a little over 150 dollars a week plus commission on the amount actually collected, in reality, I was getting commission only on the amount first raised in the estimate, and not on the actual final amount collected, which was normally more than the amount estimated! Except for the fact that I felt cheated, I did not think of making it an issue since I was only focussed on gaining experience, and getting ahead in life. After all, in India too there are companies with HR guidelines that are skewed to their advantage. However, this experience led me to advise new recruits to be alert while discussing the wages.

6

When Password Again Turned Motivator

At office too, my performance improves, and I am getting more conversions. Gidon, Shula and Nadav are happy for me and my other colleagues treat me with great respect. They too believe that I am a great performer and most of them go out of the way to impress me by offering to drop me, inviting me out for lunch or dinner and even calling me home on important occasions. Some of them now also look up to me for advice on improving their performance and whenever they face a problem, seek my inputs on finding a solution.

On the home front also, everyone is happy for me, and when I speak to Mom, I always tell her about the promise I made to myself and how serious I am about making a mark in life and doing her proud. Her reply is, "It's a good beginning but you've got a long way to go... so don't get complacent because, complacency can pull you down... and yes, don't let success get into your head... God bless you, take care."

We also have this friend of ours – his name is Rajesh but we fondly call him Uncle, who visits us only on weekends, and spends his time just playing video games. I join in on some of the games but what fascinates me is his CBR 600 bike. Since we have become good friends now, he allows me to ride the bike but strictly only around the parking lot in our complex, since I do not possess a valid driving license. My joy knows no bounds as I zoom down the pathway.

The emphasis on racing characteristics, such as a braced swingarm, centre-up exhaust system, and a more aggressive riding position adds to the thrill and excitement of riding this super machine. Occasionally, I do a wheelie or a stoppie but I desist from doing burnouts fearing wear and tear problems. The joy of riding this bike is however short lived, since Uncle is advised by some of his friends that he should not be letting me ride the bike and he goes by their advice.

Having bought a car and also yearning for a two-wheeler, I decide that now's the time to get my US driving license with both, four-wheeler and two-wheeler endorsements. I possess an Indian driving license but am not sure how much it will help in my getting a license here. I visit the Department of Motor Vehicles (DMV) office, fill up the forms and apply for a Learner's Permit. This is equivalent to the Temporary Driving License that is issued in India. I am allotted a number and when my turn comes, am given a few tests which I manage to clear. The DMV Inspector then asks me if I already have a license issued in India and when I show my license, to my pleasant surprise, he approves an Intern Driving License (IDL) valid for two months. If I had been issued a Learner's Permit, I would need to have a licensed person accompany me whenever I drive but with an IDL, I can now drive on my own. I am convinced that my lucky streak is still on.

I start driving my Ford Escort and am really enjoying it! Driving a car is so different in the US because the car is a left-hand drive and then, there is traffic discipline too. This makes driving absolutely stress-free on highways and, it is a pleasure driving on thoroughfares as well. The traffic rules are also so well formulated that there is very little scope for accidents to happen and even if they do happen, the safety features of the vehicles prevent any serious injury. Of course, all rules have to be strictly followed, and if you're pulled up for violation, you just cannot get away without paying the penalty...there's no way of trying to talk your way out.

After a couple of days, I call up the DMV office for an appointment to get my permanent license, and am asked to come the following week. On reaching the DMV office, I find that there are already a few people waiting with their car in a queue, and I too am asked to join the queue. When my turn comes, I move up to the check point with my car, and the lady inspector on duty goes around the car, checking the vehicle to see if it has all the features that are mandatory by law. She then instructs me to get in to the car for the road test, walks around, opens the right front door and gets inside the car.

I get ready to start the car and begin the road test but what happens next is totally unexpected! She says, "Just a minute... let me check the door," and tries opening the door... alas, it's jammed... it does not open... she tries hard, but it still does not open! I tell her, "You can put your hand out of the window and open it from outside" and she says, "Look young man, I know I can do that but no, that's not the way it's got to be." Yes, I had known that there was a problem with the front door and it could not be opened from inside but never for a moment did I think that opening and closing of doors would be part of the tests.

I was prepared for the test but my car had failed the test. Her contention was that any car ought to be fit enough for an emergency, and for this all doors need to be fully functional. I knew she was right and sought her advice on what I should do next, and asked her to do her best. She said, "Okay, I won't fail you... what I'll do is, extend your IDL by two months, and you can come back with a different car... better luck next time..." I felt very bad because the whole day was wasted, and I would not be receiving my wages for the day as well. Yes, my luck seemed to have taken a small break.

Fortunately for me, Bentzi, a good friend of mine offered to lend me his new Mitsubishi Galant car for my next visit to the DMV office, and for the first time, I was driving one of the most luxurious cars in the US. This time, all went well and my permanent Driving License was approved and issued.

A couple of days later, just after I reached office, I got to know that the man who had hit me and stole my money at Nadav's party was killed by the cops in a shootout. Maybe because I am an Indian and Indians are considered to be a tolerant lot, I felt bad for him, and for a couple of seconds, even prayed for him... but thinking again, it struck me that destiny probably, was playing its role... perhaps, he deserved it, and what happened to the man was just Poetic Justice.

Back in the office, orders are coming in like never before, the bottom line is getting better, and I am also able to contribute towards the overall growth of the company, by offering valuable inputs that help other departments improve their performance. Almost all my suggestions are accepted, and Gidon and Shula are fully convinced that Brunocorp stands to benefit a great deal because of me.

In the second week of February, Gidon calls me over to his cabin. When I enter, he gets up, gives me a big hug and with a smile on his face, and a look of gratitude in his eyes says, "Son, I knew you would perform but frankly I never expected you to perform so well so soon... yes, I also do know you have the potential in you to keep improving, and I am confident that you will take this company to greater heights." He pauses a while and then stretching out his hand says, "Shula and I think you deserve a promotion... from today, you take over as the Sales Manager of Brunocorp... congratulations, my son and good luck!" It was now my turn to hug him and finding it difficult to control my emotions, I said, "Thanks chief... thanks indeed...!" I was happy that the company was recognising my contribution and rewarding me for the same.

Back in my cabin, without realising that it would be late night in India, I call up Mom, and give her the good news. I am also quick to add, "Yes Mom, I remember... I will not get complacent, and I will also ensure that success does not go in to my head..." She does not respond immediately, and I think that this is because she had been sleeping but later on, I got to know that the delay in responding was because she was wiping the tears of joy. After a couple of seconds, she says, "As you cross each milestone in your career, tread cautiously so that you can continue to blaze a trail in spite of the stumbling blocks that you come across in your journey."

Later in the night, as I am in bed, I think about Gidon and Shula and I realise that they are treating me more like a son, rather than an employee, and I am moved by their love and affection. I decide that like I had promised myself about doing my Mom proud, I must also make a promise to myself that I will never let Gidon and Shula down, and that I will do all I can to stand up to their expectations. In the morning, the first thing I do after switching on my computer is to change my internet banking password to *must-do-anything4gidon*. I now have two passwords that would continue to motivate me and spur me along.

7

My First Road Trip, and All is Well

It's February end, and during a weekend party, I am introduced to Ravipraksh (RP) and his wife, Kalai who are from India. RP currently works for a leading software company in San Jose. I learn that they are a newly married couple, and RP tells me that he is trying to find a placement for his wife. As I get talking to RP and his wife, I feel as if some force within me is telling me to go ahead, and help her as she deserves to get a job. As I continue speaking with both of them, I notice that her communication skills are very strong, and she also seems capable of finding solutions to difficult problems. Back in my room, I decide that I will help her.

The next day, I speak to Gidon about Kalai and recommend her for a position in the Sales Department. "You can't be wrong... bring her along, and let me have a chat with her," says Gidon. She comes over, meets Gidon and is appointed as Sales Executive, reporting to me. I was right about her capabilities because in just three days, she picks up the tricks of the trade, and within a week of her appointment, she is already into converting orders. I am happy that I had identified the right person, and that she was capable of contributing well to the growth of the company.

In just about ten days, Kalai starts performing so well that she and I begin competing with each other on the number of calls and conversions. If I did ten converts, she would try to do more, and if she did twelve, I would try to do fifteen. It is healthy competition, and both of us are enjoying it.

We attempt different strategies to ensure optimum utilisation of both our talents – sharing the leads, timing our calls, splitting the categories of customers and so on. It is quite exciting as we try to outperform one another. Gidon too appreciates the way both of us were working as a team.

Having worked closely with Gidon and Shula for over two months now, I also get familiar with some of the Jewish rituals, and one of the rituals, the observance of Shabbat, has a direct impact on the moving business. For a 24-hour period from Friday evenings to Saturday evenings, the Jews refrain from working and engage only in prayer, fasting and other restful activities. As such, during this shut-down period, there is a heavy demand for moving companies that are working. Naturally, Kalai and I work overtime during this period and try to increase the orders for our company. Both of us try to identify similar situations and try to outperform each other.

Around the middle of March, I remembered that my return ticket to India was soon to expire and I also remembered that I needed to be in Chennai when Simbu's movie, *Kuththu*, was being released on April 14th, the Tamil New Year's day. Simbu had already seen success as a child artiste but this movie casting him as a teenager for the first time was very important to him. His future in films would depend on how successful the movie was and the entire Tamil film industry too was waiting to see how Simbu had performed. Further, I had always made it a point to be with Simbu whenever his movies were released and it had always been a practice for both of us to visit the theatre on the first day of the release of his movies, just to watch the audience reaction. We just loved it.

So, I tell Gidon that I had to take a couple of days off and he says okay but allows only eighteen days leave. He also agrees to reimburse my Chennai-San Jose return trip. I already have my San Jose-Chennai tickets and Gidon's offer is a great thing.

I confirm my ticket for 1st April and as I am preparing to leave, back of my mind, Kalai's performance seemed to be disturbing me for the first time... would she perform better than me... would Gidon decide that I had done enough for Sales and that I needed to move to some other department... would he give me a more responsible job to do... all these questions start coming up. Now, however, I am confident that I can handle any situation and I am determined that, whatever responsibility I am given, I would gladly accept and just go about proving myself.

I leave for India and even though it's just been about three months since I left the country, as I land in Chennai International Airport on 2nd April, I feel almost similar to how I felt when I first landed in the US. I meet up with all my loved ones, spend hours together trying to make up for lost time, get updates on the scene in Chennai... and, even before I can realise, it is 14th April, the date of Simbu's movie release. In time to catch the first day first show audience reaction, Simbu and I ride on a bike to the theatre and even before we enter, we can see that the movie is a big hit! The audience reaction is just amazing! I congratulate Simbu and feel so happy for him. I know he has a great future in films.

On 18th morning I am on the flight back to San Jose and as I relax, I start thinking about the next phase in my career... is Kalai continuing to perform well... does Gidon have anything else lined up for me... again, I assure myself that all is going to be well and I will take it as it comes.

When I'm back in the office, I notice that Kalai has indeed been doing very well and in fact, has been performing better than how I had performed. While I am happy for her, I also have a vague feeling that my progress could be slowed down because of her performance. In the afternoon, at about 2.30, Gidon calls me over and coming straight to the point asks me "Son, I have observed your interest in trucks... how much do you like trucks...?" Obviously, he had seen me talking to the drivers during lunch breaks and also noticed my interest in the vehicles. "I like trucks as much as I love cars and bikes,' I say. He then asks me "How would you like to also take to driving the trucks once in a way in addition to handling your sales responsibilities... you'll make yourself a thousand dollars per day when you drive...?"

I do some quick thinking... a thousand dollars per day as against two hundred dollars per week; the thrill of driving long distance on scenic highways; getting to travel all over the country; and who knows, a little extra money in tips as well... another challenge coming my way, another adventurous phase in my career journey... yes, why not?

"Look son, at any point of time, if you feel you can't handle it, you're welcome to come back full time to sales..." he continues. "I'll do it Gidon... it's right down my alley, and let me assure you, I can not only handle it but I'll do much better than you expect me to do... it's a promise." Maybe my expression, or the way I said it exuded my confidence, and the look on Gidon's face changed from one of scepticism to one of appreciation. "Come along" Gidon said, and we both walked down to where the trucks were parked.

"Go on, get in, do a small test drive and get a feel of it," he said.

It is a manual shift, 28' box truck and with a little manipulation, I am able to handle it. I drive round the block and the test drive takes just about ten minutes. Gidon is satisfied and very impressed with the way I shifted the gears smoothly and he is convinced that I can do it. To me, it felt as if I just had to put in a little more effort than I normally put when driving my SUV back home. I know that with time, driving trucks would become as easy as driving a car. Now, I had to get my Medical Card issued by a Government approved doctor in order to be able to drive trucks for local moves. A colleague recommends a Chinese doctor down the street and I get the Card.

On 23rd April, a day before my birthday, Gidon shows me a brand new truck in the parking lot, introduces me to an American, a six footer, who is a Helper and, tells me that I need to get ready to drive down to Monterey which is a distance of about 120 kilometres. My helper too is new to the job and I feel a wee bit comfortable because of this. I am handed over the details of the customer and my helper and I settle down for the drive that would take me a little more than an hour by the 101 highway via Gilroy and Salinas. I am conscious that this is my first trip as a truck driver and that I am in control of a brand new truck. Gidon wishes me good luck and like back home in India, I say a small prayer before I set off.

There's no GPS and all I have is a Thomas Guide, a spiral bound atlas with a comprehensive index of all streets in addition to arterial maps of specific metropolitan areas. The journey passes off without any incident but when we reach our destination in Monterey, we find that the job is much bigger than estimated and with eight hundred boxes to handle, it takes my helper and me eight hours to finish. The customer is happy and gives us both a tip of a hundred dollars each. I treasure the tip and realise that if you work hard, you can, indeed, make good money.

8

The Moves Continue, it's a Learning Experience all the Way

Just as we leave Monterey, Gidon calls to tell me that we have a second job on hand, a local move in San Jose. I say okay but since both of us are tired, I request for another helper. When we are back in San Jose and drive down to the customer's place, I find that it's a third floor apartment and since there is no elevator, we need to climb forty two steps to reach the apartment. Further, even though it's just a ten kilometre shift distance, it's a fully furnished two bedroom apartment and we need to pack, load and then unload... it's already 6 p.m. and with just two of us, it might take more than 12 hours. In the meantime, Shula has brought a new helper and introduces him to me. His name is Juan and he is from Mexico which means, he can speak and understand only Spanish... and, neither I nor my helper can speak Spanish!

We get down to work and while all three of us are involved in the packing, I decide to ask Juan to carry the boxes. Since I am not sure how I ought to communicate this to him, I tell him, "Just take the boxes," at the same time, gesticulating with my hands so that he understands. Without a word, Juan starts carrying the boxes from the apartment to the truck, climbing up and down the forty two steps and when he has finished, he looks weary and worn out. I begin to wonder if I had done right in asking him to handle the boxes by himself... maybe, I too ought to have chipped in... but I was so tired! It's 4 in the morning when we finish the move and we are given a tip of three hundred dollars which we split between the three of us. So, that makes it a total of two hundred dollars in tips for me... a good reward at the end of a hard day's work.

I get back to office, park the truck and getting into my car, head home. I am exhausted and I check my time... it's 4.30 in the morning of 24th April... gosh, it's my birthday! After parking my car in the garage at home, I check out my mobile for calls only to find that the charge is down... I feel exhausted and just go to bed and in minutes, fall asleep.

After just four hours sleep, I wake up at about 8.30 a.m. and I notice that all my friends have a grim look on their faces. I get to know that they had invited over thirty friends and together, had decided to celebrate my birthday in a grand manner... and I had disappointed them! I am moved by their gesture and apologise, and also tell them that dinner will be on me tonight.

I then call Mom and after wishing me on my birthday, with concern in her voice she asks, "Is it very difficult... are you sure you are not straining yourself too much... take care of your health and do ensure that you eat healthy food at the appropriate time." I assure her that I am enjoying myself. She then goes on to tell me that she has arranged for a *homam* at the temple and suggests that I too visit a temple. I tell her "For me your blessings have as much sanctity as God's blessings... thanks Mom... bye."

On 27th April Gidon calls me over and tells me "Look my son, nobody seems to want to work with you when you're driving." I don't understand what he is trying to convey. He goes on "I suggest you do a moving job tomorrow as a Helper... Kaviel will be on the trip with you. He's been working with me for about six years now and you'll sure learn a lot from him on how to handle the job better." I don't ask Gidon anything... I just tell him "Sure Gidon, whatever you say."

The next day I go with Kaviel and I do the boxes. As I watch him work, I am amazed at the precision with which he handles the whole job... absolutely professional. No wastage of time, no wrong moves, proper allocation of work, in total control of what he is doing, and going about his work with ease and perfect timing. This is a new experience for me... I learn a lot on this trip, and I realise how much better I could have done on my first trip with Juan.

Back in the office, Gidon asks me "How did it go son...?" and I tell him, "Well, I learnt a lot... thanks Gidon, for the opportunity." Gidon then asks me if I noticed how I was treated as a Helper and then goes on to say, "Juan who was the helper on your first trip has eight years' experience and you made him do all the boxes... you were not supposed to because, guys with so much experience must not be asked to carry all the boxes alone." I repented for what I had done and explained to Gidon that I was not aware of this and since Juan did not speak English and I could not communicate in Spanish, I seemed to have made a mistake.

I repented for what I had done to Juan and to make amends, I got to learn how to say 'I'm sorry' in Spanish and made it a point to meet Juan and tell him so. The way he looked at me and the way he shook my hands, I knew all was forgotten. I had learnt one more lesson... get to know more about colleagues and treat them with the respect they deserve.

I continued to do well in Sales as well, and at one stage with the volume of business increasing by almost four times,

I observed that the Operations chief was not able to handle the volume of business. Driving trucks and undertaking moving assignments gave me an opportunity to interact with professionals in the moving industry and this, in turn, gave me a better insight into the core principles of cost effective operations. A lot of simple but effective tips that I got also helped me understand the business better.

For example, one day I took a break while driving and picked up a conversation with a driver who was changing his tyre. He was experienced and much older than me. As we got talking, I asked him to advise me on how I could become a more professional driver, and one of the things he told me was "if you want to really do good for your company, the lesser number of times you open the truck door, the more your profits." What he meant was that I should plan and time my trips in such a way that I don't waste time taking too many breaks. This was an excellent tip and as I began practising this, I found that I could save so much time and in the process, increase the billing too!

Now, here was an opportunity for me to do my bit in helping the Operations department at Brunocorp by using the knowledge and experience that I had gained. Gidon, as usual, gave me the okay and I began to streamline the operations by implementing simple measures related to time management, cost effective route planning, optimum utilisation of manpower and better personnel management. My strategies worked... the Operations department improved and got geared up to handle large volumes of business. Gidon and Shula were overwhelmed with my continued success and with the bottom line getting better and better, their joy knew no bounds. Whatever I did seemed to be right and financially too, I was doing well.

A couple of days later, when I am deputed to go on a trip, I reach office and find that Jobi, the Foreman, has reported sick. Gidon asks me to handle the job and now, instead of one truck and two people, I am in charge of five trucks and eleven people. The job is worth twelve thousand dollars and it would be 1500 dollars in tips. I manage perfectly and ensure that the final billing is much more than anticipated.

Another trip I remember was when I went to Los Angeles. I drove to LA in six hours, completed the job in three hours and immediately drove back to San Jose in six hours. The total time I took was just fifteen hours. Gidon was highly impressed because this was the first time a driver had returned from LA without taking a break and staying overnight in a hotel... I not only saved time but also saved a lot of money for the company, and above all, the truck could be used for another trip and this, in turn, would bring additional revenue. Gidon was so impressed with my dedication and application of mind to the job that he increased my allowance from twenty cents to twenty five cents a mile.

Then, on another trip, I was driving all alone on a plain in Corpus Christi, a coastal city in the South Texas region of the U.S. state of Texas. It was 4 a.m. and raining, and I suddenly found the truck skidding and I had absolutely no control. It continued to skid for just a few seconds before I was able to get it on course, but I can tell you, those few seconds were scary. It was a first time experience for me and it took me quite some time before I could get back to normal.

9

Setting my Sights on a Ferrari

Then again, I will never forget one of the trips when I was returning from Texas. I had just entered the Mexico Main Station area when I was pulled up by the cops. After checking my papers, they went on to check my log book and told me that since I had been driving for more than the number of hours as stipulated by the law, I need to park and rest overnight. I knew they were wrong but without arguing, I parked and tried to locate a hotel to spend the night.

As I lay asleep, around 1 a.m., I got a call from Gidon informing me that he had received information about the truck having damaged a barricade. Something told me that the cops were trying to frame me and so, after reaching the station, without going anywhere near the truck, I first informed the cops that I was the driver and asked them if they could check out. I reached the truck along with the cops and noticed that the truck had moved forward and hit against the barricade. The first thing the cops did was to open the door and check if the hand brake was up... it was, but they tried telling me that it was not! However, since it was clearly visible and obvious that the hand break was indeed up, they decided not to press charges against me.

The cops spent about fifteen minutes around the truck trying to find out if there was anything else that they could pin on me but since they could not, they just said "Just get the truck out of here..." I started the truck, drove to the hotel and after picking up my luggage, headed back to San Jose. I parked the truck in the office, went home and just slept.

Gidon and the rest of the staff thought that I would need to sort out the problem at Mexico, stay overnight and return only the next day and so when they found the truck parked outside, they were surprised. When I entered the office, Gidon was astonished and patting me on my back said, "You're simply outstanding... you handled it exceptionally well... great job, my son."

I now decided to change my car and since I was travelling frequently on long distance trips and not using the car regularly, I wanted a car with manual shift so that I could always push and start it in case the battery dies. I looked up the website again and a black two-door Honda CRX 1990 hatchback caught my attention. I managed to find a buyer for my present car, and this time too, I asked Nadav to join me and we went in his car.

As we drove, we passed a Ferrari showroom and I just couldn't take my eyes off the Italian beauties parked there. I had always wanted to own a Ferrari but whenever such a thought came to my mind, I had always looked at it as a distant dream waiting to be fulfilled. Now, I asked Nadav to pull over near the Ferrari showroom and pointing to the Ferrari's parked inside, told him "You know what, in another two years, one of those cars is going to be mine..." and I gave him a smile. Nadav smiled back and I knew he was not taking me seriously. He was probably wondering how I could think of a car that costs 170,000 dollars when I was able to just about afford a car for 750 dollars. I went on, "Yes, and when I buy a Ferrari in two years, even if we are not working together, wherever you are, I promise to call and inform you." I took delivery of the Honda CRX and Nadav and I went out for dinner that night.

One very good thing about Gidon was that he always believed in rewarding good performance and whenever the team performed well, he used to celebrate in one way or the other. It was on one such occasion that Gidon decided the entire staff should celebrate and party at the Lake Anderson in San Jose. Catering was arranged, there were fun-filled events and above all, there was jet skiing too.

As we were all enjoying ourselves, we suddenly heard a loud cry. The Jet Ski that one of our colleagues in the Sales Department was riding had flipped; he was thrown off and in the impact, fractured his leg. He was probably riding at a high speed or he was not aware that while making a turn sharper than 90 degrees while riding a Jet Ski, you must not slow down but continue to maintain acceleration. We immediately packed up and rushed him to the hospital. Fortunately, it was a simple fracture and he recovered soon.

Just prior to buying my second car, I had sold my Ford Escort to a colleague's friend and memories of the car began fading away. However, a couple of days after I had sold the car, I started receiving legal notices from the DMV asking me to pay a penalty. The buyer of my car had been pulled up and found driving without a valid license and since the DMV had no record of my having sold the car, I was answerable. Only then did I get to know that in the US, when you sell your car, you need to inform the DMV within five days of the sale, and also mail a Release of Liability form so that you are not held responsible for any illegal issues related to the car, that may arise after the sale.

Meanwhile, my younger brother Anand who has just graduated in Architecture decides to join me in the US as he too is keen on a career here. Mom calls me up and asks me whether I can manage if Anand comes over. I assure her that that I am fairly well settled in my job and my income too is okay and there is absolutely no problem.

Anand flies in and I receive him at the airport. I have kept my friends informed about his arrival and have also told them that he too would be staying with us. For the first few days after his arrival, I show Anand around and we visit all the tourist spots in San Jose. I am aware that he may not be able to make much headway as an architect in the US and so as we discuss on the future course of action. I also know that since Anand likes to keep to himself and normally does not mix, he will not be able to take up sales or marketing as a career.

Anand is 5'6" and is not very muscular built and so I am apprehensive as to whether he will be able to handle truck driving. However, with not many options available, I ask him if he would like to join me as a truck driver. Initially he hesitates but after I explain to him about the job and tell him how it has been for me, he agrees to try it out.

My next move is to first get Anand his basic Driver's License. He clears the tests in the first attempt and when he's back in the room, narrates how the test went off and how he managed it. His narrative reminds me of how, after returning from school, he used to start giving Mom and me a detailed description of everything that had happened during the day and if he found that we were not listening, he would get up, go and sit in a corner of the room and stay put there till we made up and lent our ears. Even during our school days, I just couldn't bear to see him upset and now too, I decided that I would never give him a chance to feel sad or unhappy... I would always make things easy for him.

I told myself that if Anand and I were together deputed on moving assignments, I would carry the heavy stuff and let him do the easy tasks.

After about a week, I begin to notice that my friends do not seem to be happy about Anand staying with me. I get to overhear snide remarks being made about my bringing people over from India and putting them up with me and also as to how much discomfort this is causing my friends. It hurts, because I always thought that good friends do not stand on etiquette... and it also hurts a lot more because my brother is made to feel guilty.

Anand and I ponder over the situation, I try to comfort him but I can see that he is teary eyed and is possibly thinking that his coming over has made things difficult for me. I too am unable to hold on to my tears but for Anand's sake, I put on a brave face and tell him, "Look Anand... things are going to be okay... Mom's blessings are with us and we'll find a way out very soon." Even though I said this more to comfort Anand, deep inside I was confident that this time too, things would indeed work out well for us and fall in place.

I go on to tell Anand that we should always value friendship in life and as someone had said, "Good friends are hard to find, harder to leave and impossible to forget." "Maybe, we are destined for something better," I tell him. So, we decide not to make it an issue with our friends and also look for options that would solve the problem. We tell our friends that we are sorry about the inconvenience and that both of us would be moving out soon.

Anand too starts looking at the problem with a different perspective and quickly gets back to his normal happy self.

We speak to Mom and tell her what's happened and she assures us that whatever is happening is only for our good. She also asks me if I had watched the video clipping of the *Homam* she had performed on my birthday and I confess that I had not and that I would very soon.

10

Going it Alone... a Prelude to Disaster

Over the next few days, Anand and I look at the Real Estate ads in newspapers and also keep all our friends informed about our requirement but we can't find any accommodation. Then, I decide to look up the website again and to our luck, see a classified ad about a one-room accommodation available in Milpitas itself. We go over and find that an Indian couple with one child own the town house. After checking out on our antecedents and getting to know more about us, they agree to rent out a small room in their town house for five hundred dollars a month.

Since we had decided not to make it an issue with our friends, they too reciprocate well and see to it that we part as good friends, and also promise ourselves that we would continue to meet, play cricket, watch video games and have fun. I remembered the quote about friends again and yes indeed, it was harder to leave and definitely impossible to forget. I had, however, developed a sentimental attachment to the place and deep inside, I felt sad that I was moving out of such a nice place. The thought just wouldn't go away until I conscientiously made up my mind that in a few years from now, I would come back and stay here.

I had all along been concentrating only on local moves and my long distance trips were few. However, now that Anand was also there and he had also got his Medical Card, I decided that I could do more number of long distance trips with Anand accompanying me. I could travel to more cities in the US and more than that, could also improve my network with others in the industry... I would get to know the industry and the operations better. Gidon too was keen on my increasing the long distance trips since the revenue also was much more.

So, when Gidon asks me to drive down to Texas one day, I decided to take Anand along too and Gidon gives me the okay. We would be doing four thousand kilometres and the trip would take us about twenty three hours. In terms of wages, I would be making almost nine hundred dollars plus tips.

There is this rule that on long distance assignments, one can drive for eleven hours without taking a break or drive and work on a trip for fourteen hours. Beyond the fourteen hours, one was permitted to sleep in the truck but only if it had a bed with a provision to place a pillow...if not, one had to take a room in a hotel.

It is night when Anand and I leave San Jose and it's raining too. Both of us drive in turns and maintain a log book to record the entire trip. We pass through Salinas which lies east-south east of the mouth of the Salinas river at an elevation of 52 feet above sea, continue via Las Banos, Gilroy, Baskerville, Barstow, Arizona and reach Oklahoma which has a picturesque landscape that includes the Great Plains, mountains, forests and lakes. We are at our destination in twenty two hours.

When preparing for the return journey, I am informed by Gidon that we would be returning empty! No way... I have got to do something, I tell myself. I do not wait to inform Gidon but start making cold calls on my mobile to some of my contacts in other moving companies and check if they have loads for San Jose. I also offer a discounted rate on the tariff. My efforts pay off and luckily for me, I manage to pick up and drop material all along the return journey.

When we reach the office, I hand over Gidon the total collection of seven thousand dollars and he is surprised because I had earned the company an extra three thousand dollars...and, I had done it out of sheer presence of mind and by going that extra mile. I felt I was only paying back Gidon and Shula for all the trust and confidence they reposed in me and also for all the love they showered on me. The password too was having the desired effect. An overwhelmed Gidon gave me a big hug and said "You never stop surprising me... God bless you my son."

Anand and I continued to do long distance trips together and again, every trip was a learning experience for me. On our drives to New York, the rules permitted us to take only the Express Highways and not the Parkways, and the former had very limited or restricted access for trucks. Violation could result in a ten thousand dollar fine and a thirty-day layoff. I also learnt that toll fees had to be paid on many stretches even if it was not a highway and sometimes, the total toll fees between San Jose and New York would work out to as much as seven hundred dollars.

Then, I remember that on another trip to New York, it was late night and we had parked the truck and gone to sleep after we had reached Pennsylvania. Early in the morning at about 4 a.m., I woke up and noticed that the truck seemed to be moving, and I just could not control the movement. I got nervous and woke up Anand and told him what was happening. He looked out and after a moment started laughing out.

What actually happened was that the trucks on either side of us were moving and even though we were stationary, this had made me feel that our truck was moving... just like it happens when you park your car at a signal and when the car next to you moves a bit ahead, you get the feel that your car is going in the reverse. Anyway, I realised that because I was not resting enough, my reaction to situations seemed to be distorted and decided that henceforth, I would ensure sufficient rest on all trips.

The summer season was just around the corner and the demand for local moves started increasing. Going by past experience, I knew that most of the local moves happened either during the beginning or the end of the month. As such, I worked out our trip schedule in such a way that Anand and I travelled long distance during the middle of the month, and worked on local moves during the beginning and end of the months. On an average, we were able to do about four local moves in a day and inclusive of tips, I could earn almost nine hundred dollars per day.

As days passed by, the demand for long distance trips also started increasing and Gidon felt that it was time I did a long distance trip without Anand accompanying me. He felt that Anand was now capable of doing it alone and as such, if this was done, it would mean extra revenue for the company. Anand is a person who accepts challenges just to prove a point... he believes that if someone else could achieve something, he too could. Even as a child, he had this trait in him and our parents and I thought this was good for him because this inner urge to compete and succeed would do him good in life. In this case too, I was sure that Anand would agree to do a long distance trip alone, even if it was only to prove to himself and others that he could do it. Nevertheless, I checked out with him and he agreed.

It was a Monday morning and Gidon informed me that I would have to leave for New York the next day and this time, Anand would not be accompanying me. Anand would be on his own and since the truck meant for him had not yet come in, I would be leaving first. It suddenly dawns on me that Anand will be doing his first trip on a Tuesday and even though I am not very superstitious, I am concerned, but cannot do anything about it. The next day, I tell Anand to drive cautiously, and also adhere to all safety regulations... I then wish him good luck on his maiden solo trip and commence my journey.

My mobile phone, a few energy bars and Red Bull cans are my constant companions on every journey and on this trip too, as I go along, I munch on an energy bar and focus on my path ahead. At about 10.30 p.m. California time, Anand calls me up to say that he is all set to drive on his first solo trip and his destination too is New York. I wish him good luck once again and tell him that since I will be returning from New York and we would cross paths half way, we can exchange places... he can take my loaded truck to San Jose and I could take his loaded truck to New York. I wanted to do this because I knew Anand would be unable to physically unload the goods all by himself and I wanted to spare him the task.

As I continue on my journey, I decide to drive through smaller and less congested streets and as I do so, realise that it is beginning to get pitch dark and there are no road lights either. I pick up my phone but the tower signals are very weak... I can neither make nor receive calls. I also observe that I am alone and my truck seems to be the only vehicle on the road... there is absolutely no movement of other vehicles on the stretch. I tell myself that rather than continue to drive, taking a break would be a more sensible thing to do. A few kilometres ahead, I see a gas station that is closed and I decide to park inside. As I close my eyes and try to get some sleep, an eerie feeling and a sense of foreboding passes through me... I shrug it off and blame it on fatigue.

11

Down a Cliff but Thank God

After a disturbed sleep, I wake up at about 4.30 a.m. I check my phone and find that it is working and as I do so, I note that there have been quite a few missed calls... from Anand, from Gidon, from Nadav and from a couple of my other colleagues. All of them seemed to have been desperate to reach me. Worried and nervous, I brace myself and call Gidon and he tells me, "Son, your brother met with an accident and we tried reaching you... the truck he was driving toppled down a cliff in Fairfield!" I wait with bated breath not knowing what's coming next, and he goes on, "But don't worry, nothing has happened to him... he is safe and thank God, has only minor injuries." I then get to know that fortunately, at that point of time, fire engines were parked close by and they rushed to the site and managed to save Anand. The truck was mangled almost beyond recognition.

I try calling Anand but obviously, he is in a state of shock and possibly, also feeling terribly guilty and upset over the accident as well as the consequences. The financial loss to the company, the severe damage to the truck, the compensation that needed to be paid to the customer, the influence it would have on Gidon's relationship with me... all these thoughts are possibly disturbing him and he is not in a state of mind to speak with me. I do not insist on him speaking with me.

Shaken, but happy that Anand was safe, I continue to drive on to New York and after unloading, load another consignment and immediately head back to San Jose telling myself that there would be absolutely no breaks in between, since I am eager to get back and see Anand. After driving about eight hours non-stop however, I decide to take a break at Cleveland in Ohio. As I get out of the truck and look at the vast expanse of the plains in front of me, I think about the twists and turns in my life and think about all that had happened since I landed in the US... I am reminded of my uncle's words and Mom's advice. I turn up and look at the skies and see a rainbow... and, something tells me that I must not lose confidence, and that better times are in store for me.

After a short break, I get back on to the truck and resume my journey. Whenever I drive, I have this habit of visualizing God and Mom guiding me... God in the front leading me ahead and Mom in the rear, cheering me on and now too, as I begin to think about Anand's future, it is God and Mom that seem to be guiding me and I continue with renewed vigour in spite of a hard day behind me.

When I get back and meet Anand, his face reveals the turmoil he has been going through... I just hold his hand and tell him, "Look Anand, just think of the accident as a bad dream... and that you have just woken up from it... just forget it... everything can be taken care of... just leave it to me and relax." Tears well up in Anand's eyes and tightening the grip on my hands he says "No anna, I know I have let you down... I've been thinking about it and I believe that the best thing I can do is to give up on moving as a career... at least this way, there would be no chance to hurt you again..." I don't know how to react and when I ask him, "Are you sure da...?" he replies with a determined "Absolutely sure!" I know that Anand always thinks about the pros and cons and gives it a lot of thought when taking a decision but once he decides, he sticks to it. I think that letting him have his way is the best thing I can do.

Anand wants to get into architecture and I tell him to take all the time he needed to find the right job. After all, he could use my car, he had a laptop and we were staying together... there was nothing to lose. Fortunately, he recovers from the shock quickly and in a week's time, gets a job in an architect's office, and soon things start looking up for him.

Gidon tells me that I have to compensate for the damages of fifteen thousand dollars due to Anand's accident and when I remind him that the truck was covered by insurance, he says, "If we do get the insurance I'll give you back the money." I agree to Gidon deducting three thousand dollars from my salary every month... again, I really do not mind because I'm here to learn, learn and just learn... money is not a big deal.

Meanwhile, in June, Gidon's relative named Shuki joins the company. His intention is to learn on the job and gain some work experience so that he is equipped to pursue a successful career. The first time he is introduced to me, something tells me that we will not vibe well with each other and over the next few days, his body language as well as the way in which he carries himself does not impress me at all. I decide to keep him at arm's length. A short while after Shuki joins the company, I notice that he begins to exceed his brief and tries to get Gidon to change established procedures. Every move that Gidon make's on Shuki's advice proves to be a big disaster and over a period of time Gidon stops acting on his advice and sees to it that he just does what he is supposed to do, that is, observe and learn.

With the number of orders as well as the volume of consignments to be moved increasing, Gidon suggests that

I start driving the bigger 18-wheeler trucks which would enable three truck loads to be moved on every single trip. Obviously, increased loads would translate into bringing in more revenue, and since increasing revenues for the company was on my agenda too, I agree.

Now, in order to drive the bigger trucks, I needed to get the Class A Commercial Driving License (CDL) and if I got this with all endorsements, I would be authorised to drive any kind of heavy vehicle including ambulances and fire-fighting trucks. In relation to the bigger trucks used for moving goods, I would be able to drive any combination of vehicles with a Gross Vehicle Weight Rating (GVWR) of 26000 pounds or more, that is almost 12000 kilos, as long as the vehicle being towed weighs more than 1000 pounds, that is almost 500 kilos.

But before I applied for the Class A CDL to the Department of Motor Vehicles (DMV), I had to get properly trained at a Government approved Driving School for four hours a day for two weeks, and this would cost three thousand dollars! At the school, I would be taught the required skills and knowledge to pass a series of tests. Gidon agreed to pay the amount and treat this as an advance, and the company would deduct a specified sum from my salary every month. A fair deal, I thought.

After completing the training I had to take a theory and practical test, the former consisting of over 160 questions on subjects including the Air Brakes Practice Test, the Combination Vehicles Test and so on. Since I was basically interested in trucks and I was genuinely interested in learning whatever there was to learn about trucks, I considered the training as more of a learning experience rather than a painful exercise. I worked very hard, prayed devotedly, invoked my mother's blessings... and, at the end of it, I cleared both the tests in the first attempt itself. I got to know later that most of the persons attempting the tests, manage to clear it in two or three attempts.

Now that I had got my Class A CDL and was authorised to drive bigger trucks, I knew that Gidon would soon decide on getting me to drive a bigger truck and I had to be ready. One day, as I was browsing the net, I got to know that the cost of leasing trucks in Texas was much lesser than what they cost in California. I discussed this with Gidon and told him that we ought to be getting the trucks from Texas. He wanted to make sure if could handle the big trucks and I said I could. He suggested that we go in for a 53' truck but I told him that I would prefer to begin by driving a 28' truck and he agreed.

I flew to Texas to meet up with the sales team at Vibrant Truck Leasing Corp in Houston. It was a holiday but as luck would have it or shall I say, my destiny had planned it, a senior official came, opened the office and within a short time, the contract was signed and I was handed over the keys of a 28,' eighteen-gear Kenworth truck with three gear shifts. I did a test drive but found the gears a bit difficult to manipulate. I asked for a lighter truck and was shown an International truck, manufactured by the International Truck and Engine Corporation. This truck had ten gears and even though it lacked the luxuries that the Kenworth truck provided, it was light and I had no problem with the gears. I took delivery of the truck and headed back to California. It was to be a 2300 kilometre drive and would be taking me about 24 hours. Before I started on my journey, as usual, I remembered to say a small prayer and also invoked Mom's blessings.

12

A Bright Dawn but a Dark Day

I take the i10 highway via El Paso and Phoenix but while driving through Barstow which is about 600 kilometres before San Jose, I don't realise that I am over speeding and doing 120 kmph as against the limit of 90 kmph. I get a ticket, pay the penalty and continue on the final lap of my journey. When I reach office, Gidon and the rest of the staff are waiting to receive me and they all go gaga over the new truck... it's celebration time!

Having made a beginning in doing long distance trips driving bigger trucks, I also become conscious of the fact that, thanks to my wages of forty cents per cubic foot plus other allowances and tips, my income levels too are going up and now, I can look out for a bigger place to stay. In a flash, I remember that just the other day, Gidon, had casually mentioned to a customer that there was an apartment available for rent in the residential complex where he was staying. Was it a coincidence or was it destiny continuing to lead me on my path to success...? To me, it looked like the latter.

Anand and I visit the place on to check it out. It is a one bedroom apartment and also has a small storeroom that could be used as a second bedroom. There is provision for a small puja room too and since I chant the Hanuman Chalisa devotional hymn regularly, and am also a devout Hindu, the place seems just right for me. The complex also has a swimming pool and gym. Dad was planning to visit us too and this, I thought, was the right time to shift. On

September 10th, in the midst of a 36-hour break for me, we move in to the new place and now, Gidon is our neighbour. A couple of days after we shift, Dad comes down and Dad, Anand and I spend a lot of precious moments together.

My first trip after taking delivery of the new truck is to New York and I take the Interstate80 highway, commonly known as the I80. Now, since I'm driving a much bigger truck, it takes a little more effort on my part to handle the turns and I have to do a lot of calculated thinking to gauge the distances and amount of space available when I back up or park. It's both, fun and caution.

The Thomas Guide is at hand and the drive takes me through many important cities like Nebraska, Iowa and Ohio. Keeping me company as usual, is my Red Bull, mobile phone and a few energy bars as well. It's a forty-two hour drive and half way through, as I get to feel lonely, I call up Mom and my friends in between breaks and have long conversations. During one of the calls, Mom is having lunch and tells me that she had been just thinking about me as she had cooked my favourite chicken biryani and chilli fish... my taste buds are tickled, and I head for the nearest fast food outlet.

On all my trips, in addition to speaking to my family and friends, I also speak to my contacts in the moving industry just to keep abreast of the business related developments. In whichever city I have halted, I make it a point to talk to the other drivers, the helpers and to senior personnel of other moving companies. Fortunately for me, I am able to develop a good rapport with whoever I meet and as such, am able to establish a good network of contacts. My contacts also seem to be impressed with my disciplined working, dedication and cost effective operations.

On my return trip from New York, I find that I don't have a load from Texas to California. I almost feel guilty about it and something tells me that there is an opportunity waiting to be taken and if I try hard, I will be able to get a consignment. I give it a thought and then, decide to call up some of my contacts in other companies to check if they had any orders to California. The second call I make proves to be lucky and I get a load... and, when I get back to San Jose, Gidon expects me to hand over twelve thousand dollars but I give him twenty eight thousand dollars in cash... yes, twenty eight thousand as against twelve thousand. He just can't believe it! This is a first-time occurrence for him and never before, in his whole career, has he ever been given anything more than the routine collection.

I am exhausted and I freshen up and order for a Cappuccino. After finishing my coffee and as I decide to leave for the day, Gidon calls me and hands over my wages... and guess what... no, he does not reward me with extra money... guess again, no, he does not offer me a promotion... well, I bet you can't guess... he has, in fact, deducted three thousand dollars towards the fifteen thousand dollars I owe him! I don't feel bad because I owe him the money anyway and I'm here to learn and move ahead... money, for me, at this point of time is just incidental... end of the day, I am happy for Gidon and pleased with myself for what I had done for the company.

Even on my first trip, I realise that the truck's pre-set speed governor which restricts the speed to 120 kilometres per hour is a big hindrance as I am unable to drive on stretches which have a speed limit of 130 kilometres or even more. As such, when I get back to base, I speak to one of my friends, a professional and experienced truck mechanic, and he manages to change the settings so that I am able to drive at higher speeds.

On my next trip with the 18-wheeler truck, as I drive from California to New York I decide to attempt a higher speed on the 640-kilometre stretch in Wyoming and I am able to do this in just about 3 ½ hours at a speed of about 180 kilometres per hour.

I am informed that my next trip, the second with the 52' truck, will be to Virginia. I am also told that this is job has been pending for a long time and I need to handle the customer with care since he is already very upset over the delay. It's a long drive that could take about forty hours and I begin the trip on alert mode and prepare myself for the fireworks.

Just about two hours into the drive, at Coalinga, I notice a truck that has been pulled up by the cops and as I pass by, I do everything possible to escape the attention of the cops... but no, one of them is already in front of me, displaying a yellow sign asking me to pull over! He tells me that I was over speeding and yes, gives me a ticket! A customer who is waiting to take it out on me and now, a ticket... something tells me that this trip was going to be eventful for the wrong reasons and I choose to just park at the nearest pit stop and sleep.

After a good sleep, I resume my journey to Virginia, take the Interstate 5 highway and drive through Arizona, New Mexico, Oklahoma, Mississippi and Alabama. About ten hours before I am scheduled to reach Virginia, I call up and outsource the service of four helpers through my contacts. They are already there when I reach the customer's place and the job is completed in thirty minutes flat. I pay off the helpers and they leave.

Now, I need to collect three thousand dollars which is the balance due from the customer and so walk up to him, express regret over the delay and request him for the cash. I do not miss the wry smile on his face as he tells me that he does not have cash and offers me a Cash Cheque, which he puts in an envelope and hands over to me. As I am getting delayed for my next stop, I am in a rush to pay off the helpers and continue on the next leg of my journey... but that wry smile which I saw on the customer's face seems to be worrying me... I am almost convinced that I have made a mistake somewhere but am unable to pinpoint what it is.

It's a six-hour drive to Pennsylvania which is my next stop and as I set off, I begin to concentrate on the route I have to take and also wonder as to what else could be in store for me. As I continue to drive and take in the sights as they pass by, that wry smile keeps coming back to haunt me and I am sure that something has gone wrong... what could it be...? I keep driving... and I keep thinking... and then after about fifteen minutes, suddenly like a flash, I get it! I have forgotten to collect the signed contract from the customer and... oh my God!, I also remember that in my hurry to get the job done fast and while paying off the helpers, I had placed the envelope containing the cheque in the space between the tractor and the trailer with the intention of picking it up before I get into the truck but I had forgotten about it!

I call up the customer and tell him that I seem to have lost the cheque and ask him if he could give me another cheque. I can almost see that wry smile back again on his face as he conveys to me that as I was leaving his place, the envelope with the cheque had dropped on the floor. The sarcasm in his voice combined with the visual image of his face with that smile confirmed that he had no intention of giving the cheque back to me and I decided not to try further. Blaming myself, I call Gidon, tell him what has happened and sure enough, he points out that I would need to compensate him for the loss of three thousand dollars.

13

When Luck takes a Long Vacation

A ticket at the beginning of the trip... a loss of three thousand dollars on my first load... what next, I thought to myself. My next halt is at Pennsylvania and from the Thomas Guide I get to know that the customer's house is atop a hill. I reach the place and begin the ascent with my 52' tractor trailer. Minutes later, as I take a steep right turn, I hear a loud noise and the vehicle stops moving. On checking out, I find that while taking the turn, the tractor has hit a tree! Not wanting the customer to suffer any delay, I quickly do the unloading – it's just about fifty items – and call up Gidon to tell him what happened. He tells me that I have to get the trailer repaired at the nearest point as I am not supposed to drive with a damaged trailer. I manage to get the body repair job done at Prince and pay them two thousand dollars.

Now, I am convinced that my luck has taken a long vacation and I get on alert mode to prepare myself for any eventuality on the rest of my trip. My next halt is at Texas where I will be unloading goods at the customer's place and again, I have already outsourced four helpers to help me out. It's a 24-hour drive and as I drive, think about the incidents on the trip, but this only tires me more. So, I decide to call up some of my friends in Chennai and start chatting with them and after speaking to four of them, a better mood sets in... but will it last? I want to believe that it will, but again, as I start thinking of the day's events, I am not very sure if it will.

When I reach Texas and arrive at the customer's place, I notice that it is a billionaire's mansion. My helpers have already arrived and are waiting for me. The customer is a lady in her thirties and obviously, related to the owner of the mansion. I am very exhausted and as such, tell the helpers to go ahead and I supervise the job. At frequent intervals, however, I check and make sure the customer is happy about the handling and placement of the goods. Keeping in mind the day's events, I don't want to take any risks here. The job continues into the night and I keep my fingers crossed

It's close to midnight when the job is completed and I am happy that the customer had no occasion to complain. However, whenever she spoke to me or the helpers, I did notice that her tone indicated that she is a no-nonsense person who will have her way. I pay off the helpers and ask them to leave. Feeling relieved that the job has been completed to the customer's satisfaction, and without any unpleasant incident, I ask the customer to sign the contract and let me have the payment. As I wait for this, she makes a sweeping glance around the room... and what she does next is totally unexpected and shocking! She points to a television set that's on the floor and asks me to lift and place it on the table... I attempt doing it but try as I may, am unable to lift it. Why did she not tell me about this when the helpers were here... why can't she give me a helping hand...?

The TV set possibly weighs close to about eighty kilos and I am dog-tired... I try again but I just can't lift it. I go out and check to find out if there's anyone available to help but at this late hour, nobody seems to be there. I come back and look at her helplessly... she looks back as if like saying, "Go ahead, I'm paying you and you'd better do it!" I manage to keep my cool and determined, I tell myself that somehow, I am going to do it. What I do next is something unbelievable...

it's just like in the movies... I squat on the floor cross-legged, nudge the TV on to my lap and slowly begin to raise myself to the standing position. As my knees come up and the TV reaches the table top level, I gently move it on to the table, and ... thank God, I am done.

As I collect the cash and contract and walk back to the truck, I just can't imagine as to how one human being could treat another human being like this... was it pride?... was it ego?... or was it just attitude...? I realise that just as there are bad salesmen, there are inhuman customers too. As I continue walking back to the truck I feel a sharp pain in the back and as I climb in to the truck, I know that my back has been hurt very badly.

Since I am in Texas and because the body repair done on the trailer at Prince was just a temporary job, Gidon instructs me to drive down to Vibrant Leasing and get the repair done professionally. He also tells me that since we have insurance, we do not have to spend anything. However, when I get to Vibrant, they tell me that if the insurance amount is claimed, the accident would need to be recorded in my license and this means I would be getting yet another black mark. Otherwise, if they billed the normal way, the incident would not be recorded in my license. I did not want it go into my record and as such, asked them to send us the bill. Gidon got a bill for fifteen thousand dollars from Vibrant. He paid the amount but told me that he would be deducting this amount also from my salary! I agreed. Now I owed the company thirty five thousand dollars all put together.

Gidon continues to be impressed with everything I do, especially, my networking and time management skills. He is aware that I complete a job faster than any other driver and this means extra revenue for the company, and he is also aware that the company's interests are always top-of-mind for me. He praises me and tells me that he's never had a driver like me and that in spite of a Despatch department being non-existent in our company, I am able to handle the operations very well. I too become conscious of the fact that now, I am a big asset to the company.

Having seen success and profitability in 18-wheeler trucks, I decide that it is time we develop this as a new line of business and I discuss this with Gidon and show him how much the company stands to gain. I also speak to truck leasing companies in California, give them an indication of the volume of business that they can expect from us, and negotiate for the best rates. And, I succeed in getting rates that are much lower than the Texas based leasing companies.

We increase our fleet of trucks and because I already have a good rapport with truck drivers and other industry personnel in important cities, and since many of the truck drivers are keen to work with me, I am also able to choose and identify good drivers. We recruit Melwyn and Jacob and I brief them about how I would like them to operate. I also train them in time management and over a period of time, they adapt to my style of working and I am happy that they are doing a good job.

Just at this point of time in mid-September, Nadav decides to put down his papers. Ever since I joined the company, Nadav has been a great source of strength to me and I know I'll miss him. Gidon too is sad that Nadav is leaving as he knows he will be losing a good employee. I am happy that Nadav is planning to set up his own company along with Len, a security guard.

At the send-off party, I ask Nadav as to why he took the decision and he says "There comes a time in everyone's career when he reaches a saturation point and has three options to choose from... one, to stay on in the company and slow down or even arrest his growth, the second, to join another company and presume that he would be better off there and third, to start up on his own, be in command but also be prepared for the risks... I thought the third option suited me best..." I told myself that it was too early for me to even think of such options... but what Nadav told me did leave a mark on me and it got stored in my memory.

14

Rewards, Recognition and One Rung up the Ladder

During late September, Gidon decides to shift and we move to a much bigger office in Santa Clara which is just ten minutes from the old office. When we are there, Gidon takes me to the first floor and shows me his 10' × 10' room. We also walk down to Shula's room as well as the Sales office on the same floor. Gidon then turns to me, puts his hand on my shoulder and leading me to the ground floor says "Come, have a look at your room..." We enter the huge 40' × 30' room which also has a big desk with a swivel chair and four visitor chairs, a Mac system, three couches, a television and a huge white board, and Gidon announces "It's all yours, my son...." I'm dumbstruck!

When I look at Gidon with awe and amazement, he says, "Congratulations, you are now the Chief Operations Officer of Brunocorp...!" I just can't believe it! He goes on to tell me that since I would now have to interact regularly with all the staff of the company, I would need more space and facilities and hence, this arrangement. I now have access to all the departments, the authority to control all the staff as well as ensure streamlined operations of the company and above all, I also have the responsibility to make sure that the company's bottom line stays healthy at all times.

As soon as I reach my room, I immediately call up Mom and give her the good news about my being promoted as COO. I tell her how big my room is and also brief her on the importance of my position in the organisation. Mom is overjoyed and I can feel how much happy she is for me. We continue talking for a while and at the end says "I'm proud of you... Gidon seems to have a lot of confidence and trust in you and the only way to show your gratitude is by ensuring that you somehow match his expectations... and remember what I told you before... don't get complacent and never let it get into your head...." I assure her that I will remember and also promise her that I will continue to excel.

In October, just after we shift to the new office, Shuki, Gidon's relative, suddenly decides to leave and start his own company and surprisingly, Dekel, Jobi and Dayan from Sales, also decide to leave and join him! Gidon is visibly upset that his relative has let him down and he tries advising him but Shuki is adamant. He has been with the company for hardly four months, has possibly learnt only about twenty per cent about the business and yet, he has taken the decision to start off on his own! I am unable to understand the logic of Shuki's action. What Nadav told me at the send-off party comes to my mind and I wonder if that "appropriate" time had indeed arrived for Shuki or whether he was making a mistake and jumping the gun. Anyway, since I had never looked upon him as an achiever or a true friend, I decided to stop deliberating further about the implications of his decision to move.

Now, as Chief Operations Officer, I decide to bring in a little more professionalism into operations and as such, for the first time in the history of Brunocorp, call for a meeting of all the staff. The intention of the meeting is to demonstrate the company's willingness to involve staff in the day-to-day operations as well as to get their feedback on the present style of operations. The meeting is scheduled in my room and Gidon will be chairing the event.

As the staff troop in, I notice that many of them choose to look away from me and I attribute their behaviour to anxiety. Gidon does the welcome part and when he has finished, I take over and invite all of them to voice their views. Tea and biscuits have been served and putting on my best smile, I announce "Okay, shoot...." What happens next is something that I had least expected... one by one, each of them start taking pot-shots at me and complain that I am being partial in allocation of work and that as such, they are not getting a fair share of the jobs and wages. It is clear that their morale is low and I start wondering as to where I could have gone wrong. I had absolutely no reason to be partial and I just could not understand... I decide to stay cool, just listen to them and respond only after I have analysed their feedback. When the meeting is over, all of them exit without a word and this time again, they avoid looking at me.

At about 3 p.m. on the same day, Gidon asks me to join him in Shula's office and as soon as I go in, urges me to see the computer screen and asks, "Did you do it knowingly or unknowingly...?" I ask him to elaborate and pointing to the screen, he tells me that all the figures recorded showed that I had maintained a perfect balance in the allocation of work. There was absolutely no partiality. I request Shula to mail the details to me, rush back to my room and immediately inform all the staff that there would be another meeting tomorrow at 10 a.m. sharp and if anyone did not attend, he would be penalised. This time I tell Gidon that I would handle it myself. I then go through the figures that I had received and start preparing for tomorrow's meeting.

At the scheduled time, the staff enters my room and as they come in, noticing that Gidon is not present, glance at me trying to read my mood...it looks like they are scared that I was going to be rude to them. I put on a smile and say "Didn't expect to have you guys back so soon...am sure you didn't expect it too..." The suspense shows on their faces. I then walk up to the huge white board on which I had written all the relevant statistics, point to the figures and asked them, "Can all of you see these figures?" and all of them say "Yes." I go on... "Now look at the figures closely and please tell me where I have gone wrong..." They look at the figures... they look at me... they look at each other... and, a hush descends over the room. Analytics had thrown up the true figures in black and white and they are astounded. I then ask for the tea and biscuits to be served in buffet style and move around talking to each one of them. In the end, they are convinced that I certainly had their interests in my mind and that I would only do good for them.

My HR capabilities come to the fore once again when there's an issue with one of our drivers, Ebby. Gidon finds him unfit since he is always does a billing that is much lesser than the anticipated amount. He also finds that Ebby is lacking in initiative and proving to be a liability. Gidon asks my opinion and suggests that we may consider using him as a helper. I ask Gidon to give me two days to check out and the next day, accompany Ebby on one of his trips. To my surprise, I find that his only goal is to finish a job quickly and get back to base as fast as possible. In the process, he does not bother to pack each item and load... he just loads and randomly covers the items with whatever material that is available in the truck. This way, he is gaining in time but losing in revenue because he does not bill for packing.

Now that I have identified the problem, I explain to Gidon and tell him that I will see to it that he improves. I call Ebby, give him some pep talk, discuss the issue in detail and tell him where he is going wrong. "You have to pack every item before it goes in to the truck and you have to give the bill to the customer," I tell him sternly. I also tell him that if he goes by what I say, he will be very successful and also assure him that I shall always be there to guide him. Ebby takes my advice, follows my instructions and overnight, he changes into a thorough professional, bringing in increased revenues.

In the first week of October, Gidon needs to go to Hawaii for about two days, and knowing my love for cars, allows me to use his car, a Nissan Infiniti FX 35 SUV. The navigation is fantastic and even though I am used to reversing and parking trucks with ease, I am highly impressed with the car's back-up camera which makes parking tandem also very easy. I enjoy the experience till Gidon is back and tell myself that soon, I must change from driving a used car to owning a new car.

15

Making Headway but a Desire Unfulfilled

Now, I have additional responsibilities and we also have other drivers who can handle long distance trips but Gidon tells me that whenever there is an important local move, I must do it. I am only too happy with this arrangement since I know good money can be made even on local moves if the right assignments come my way. I am also sure that I will continue to earn by way of tips that could be as much as even a hundred dollars or more per customer.

In the US, shifting house is considered to be a very stressful experience. This is possibly because when one shifts, it involves the likelihood of a complete change in lifestyle as well as a serious effort to effectively adapt to a new environment. As such, there is always a sense of apprehension and anxiety when one moves to a new place, and this obviously causes a lot of stress. Since I am aware of this, I take all effort to ensure that the customers are relaxed during the move... I pick up a conversation, try to identify a subject of their interest, talk about it and try to get them to de-stress and unwind. Since I also know a little about Vaasthu and Feng Shui, if it's an Indian customer, I try to offer tips and friendly advice on the subject. Hence, the tips are usually high.

Sometime during mid-October, Anand feels that we need to change our car since he is not happy with the performance. Just about the same time, the person who had purchased my first car informs me that he too wants to change the car, and agrees to buy my present car, the Honda CRX.

Anand and I decide to check out the cars in a used car showroom at Fremont but there is this yearning desire in me to visit a new car showroom, not necessarily with an intention to buy but just to look at the models available and the pricing as well. So, before going to Fremont, we visit a BMW showroom that is close to our place. We are awestruck by the BMW-3 series models on display and I ask myself, why not? We then meet Wahab, the Finance Manager, just to check if I qualify for a car loan. After getting to know my employer details and other basics, Wahab says "Now, let me look at your credit rating..." There's only the gym membership recorded in my credit score and he says that this is not enough and he cannot approve a hire purchase scheme... I will not be able to buy a BMW now after all!

As I look at the cars displayed and my desire to own a BMW increases, I turn to Wahab and ask "Pal, I am very keen to buy this car...can you tell me what I should do..." and he replies, "Okay, here's what you can do... go and get yourself a used small car with EMI payment and come back to me after six months... I'll see what I can do at that point of time." I thank him and assure Anand that in six months, we would own a BMW.

We then drive down to Fremont and at the used car showroom, decide to go in for a Mitsubishi Galant 2003 model since both, Anand and I are familiar with the Indian version, the Mitsubishi Lancer we have back home in India. We make a down payment of three thousand dollars and our monthly EMI is 271 dollars. I ask Anand to drive the new car and I drive back the Honda CRX. When we reach home, I tell

Anand to mark the calendar for the same date, six months ahead.

In the U.S., it is mandatory for all moving companies to be licensed by the Public Utilities Commission (PUC) and our company is licensed and listed with the California Public Utilities Commission (CPUC). The PUC is a body which regulates the rates and services of public utilities including goods movers and a member organisation must not charge its customers more than the tariff stipulated by the PUC. There are also other guidelines which the member companies need to follow strictly. As per the PUC rules and regulations, it is also mandatory for every member company to have at least one employee, certified by the PUC, to represent the company in all its dealings with the PUC.

After Nadav has left, Gidon one day informs me that since Dekel, who used to represent the company at the PUC, has also left the organisation and no one else qualifies it, I would need to take her place and for this, I would need to pass an exam conducted by the PUC... the exam is scheduled for the next day. Fortunately, it is an open book exam which means I would be allowed to carry notes or any other material into the exam hall. The objective of the exam is to test one's ability to find and apply information and knowledge on a given subject. Gidon also hands me a big book which contains all the relevant information relating to the questions to be asked.

The next day, as scheduled I visit the PUC office on and as soon as I enter, am escorted to the exam hall by a security guard and given a big reference book, similar to the book that Gidon had given me the previous day. I am told that I have one full day to answer the twenty four questions.

Luckily for me, the questions are easy and dwell more on the basics like the number of steps in a flight of stairs, the PUC stipulated tariff etc. I answer all the questions within a short period of time and am back in the office. In about a week's time, we receive a communication from the PUC that I had passed the exam and the certification had been approved. Now I am a PUC Certified Mover and will be representing Brunocorp in all issues related to the PUC. I remember my mom's words and decide to make sure that I will concentrate only on growth and nothing else.

During the third week of October, Joy who is Gidon's cousin, joins the company as Foreman and along with him, his wife is also recruited to assist Shula in the Accounts Department. Gidon asks me to train Joy and even during the first few days of his joining, I am able to judge his capabilities and know for sure that he will not be able to handle the job well. I can also see that Joy is not opening up to me and his body language as well as his facial expressions give me the impression that he perceives me as a threat. However, I am cautious enough to refrain from giving my opinion to Gidon since Joy is his relative and he will obviously have a soft corner for him. I decide to wait and see.

Meanwhile, Simbu's movie, Manmadhan, is scheduled to be released on 11th November and as usual, I decide to be with him on that day, and book my ticket to India. This time however, Gidon does not pay for my ticket. The last time I had left for India, it was Kalai and her performance that was disturbing me. This time, as I was on the flight to Chennai, I started thinking about Joy's recruitment and the impact it could have on my standing in the organisation... would he try to impress Gidon during my absence... would he goof-up on important assignments... would he try and get a hold on the company and influence policy decisions...? All these thoughts kept coming back again and again almost half way through the flight but I tried to assure myself that just like last time, all would be well this time too. Again, like last time, this time too I was prepared for any eventuality and decided that I will face up to any challenge.

After seeing the movie in a theatre in Chennai, Simbu and I decide to fly down to Malaysia to watch the audience reaction there. The Malaysian audience is as excited about the movie as the Indian audience and the first few days of the release clearly indicate that it is going to be a big success. The movie went on to be declared as blockbuster at the box office after a run in the theatres for 275 days. Simbu's popularity grew and his fan base too increased in large numbers. I was very very happy for him.

I returned to the US during the third week of December and I could see that Joy was finding it difficult to handle the job and whenever I offered to help, he gave me a cold shoulder and assured me that he could handle it himself.

16

Another New Year, and the Journey Continues

On 1st January, 2005 I have a trip scheduled to New York and I will be taking the 18-wheeler truck. However, since my friends, Anand and I had decided to celebrate the New Year at the Milpitas apartment where I had stayed earlier, I ensure that the loading is completed on the 28th December itself. Every time we have had a weekend party at the Milpitas apartment, I used to organise the speakers and sound system for the music and this time too I ensure that our favourite music is played. The party goes on late into the night and since I oversleep, am unable leave on the trip to New York at 2 a.m. as planned. However, by 2 p.m., I am all set and ready to leave.

I say a prayer and commence my journey. As I am driving it begins to rain and just as I reach Auburn, my first point, I notice that it is snowing and boards saying 'Must carry tire chains" catch my attention. Tyre chains are normally wound around the drive wheels of a vehicle and provide maximum traction when driving through ice and snow. Since I have no chains, I am not allowed to proceed further. I have to take a U-turn to reach a store that sells tyre chains and when I go there, am told that the chains cost around five hundred dollars. I have cash just enough to cover expenses that I would incur on travel and so do not know what to do. Suddenly, an idea comes to my mind... I call up Pentan Truck Leasing and request them to arrange for payment which they do. The problem is solved.

After I buy the chains and put them on the floor of the driver's cabin, I drive on and it begins to snow heavily. This is my first winter in the US and I am enjoying every moment. As I reach the point where I had to attach the chains on to the tyres, I realize that I do not know how to do this and look around... I see a truck driver of a leading courier company attaching the chains on to his tyres and request help. I am not wearing gloves and as I take out the chains from the vehicle, it hurts quite a bit. The driver obliges and in biting cold and heavy snow, attaches the chains on to the tyres in a very short time. This problem too is solved and I continue driving at just about 16 kmph which is the permissible limit. The meter on the dashboard shows the temperature outside as minus ten degrees Celsius.

Since I am driving at a very low speed, even though I have to exercise great caution, I make sure that I take in and enjoy all the sights as well as the invigorating experience of driving through snow and ice. For the first time in my life, I see black ice which is actually a fine coating of glazed ice on the road, and since the black road can be seen below the coating, it is referred to as black ice. Oh, what an experience it is! As I drive on, I also remember the 2004 New Year's Eve... the call from Simbu... my mom's advice, my uncle's prophesying... indeed, I had come a long way since then. Thinking back, I am also amazed at the way things seem to be falling in place for me. Whenever I have faced a hurdle, I have also found a stepping stone and there seems to have been a ready solution for every problem that I have faced. It's like some invisible force has been guiding me all along.

I drive about 160 kilometres in snow with the chains attached to the tyres and at Reno in Nevada, I am told that the chains could be detached from the tyres. Again, since I am not wearing gloves, detaching the heavy chains in cold weather proves to be a painful task but I manage to do it without any serious problem.

My next stop is Michigan which is about 3300 kilometres by the i80 highway and the driving time is about 30 hours. I pass through Utah, Wyoming, Illinois and Indiana and on this trip again, like in every city that I halt for a break, I get to chat with drivers and staff of other moving companies. When I reach Michigan it is 3 a.m. and raining very heavily. Not wanting to disturb the customer at this time, I park the truck at a gas station and walk across to get a bottle of water as well as stock up on my Red Bull. Back inside the truck, I check out the time and decide to sleep a while. I remember that popular 1969 song 'Rain drops keep falling on my head' from the film 'Butch Cassidy and the Sundance Kid' and as I look at the rain and start humming the tune, fall asleep.

Suddenly I am shaken out of my sleep by a Hypnic jerk, an involuntary muscle spasm which makes you feel like you are falling, and the first thing I do is, check my watch... it is 5.30 a.m., just two hours since I went to sleep. I open my eyes, look out and – lo and behold! – I see white all around. It's been snowing heavily and everything including the truck is covered with snow – a sight I have only seen in the movies... it's just fantastic! I splash some water on my face, start the truck to resume my journey and shift gears... the truck does not budge... I look at the hand brake, look at the indicators on the dashboard and everything seems normal.

I then get out of the truck and as I check it out, see that the front left wheel of the truck is stuck in an ice wedge! I first look at it as a serious issue and a major problem but as I have always believed that it is better to light a candle than curse the darkness, I do some quick thinking to find a solution, and I think of the tyre chains. I position one of the chains in such a way that when I start the truck and shift gears, the traction of the chain enables the stuck wheel to move over the wedge... and thank God, it's over. Yet another problem, and yet another solution.

I reach the customer's place and do the unloading. He is happy and the tips are generous. My next stop is upstate New York which is situated north of New York City and the distance is about a thousand kilometres from Michigan. During the breaks I meet up with some of my contacts and I find that some of them are not happy with their jobs and are looking out, and they ask me if I can help. I promise to do my best. I also make sure I call up Mom and chat with her but the long duration breaks are reserved for a chat with my sister.

As I am nearing my destination, I get to know that the customer stays in a private home which is atop a mountain. I remember my drive above the hill at Pennsylvania and tell myself that I need to be cautious. The drive to the top is done and after I finish unloading, when I ask the customer for the exit route, to my shock and surprise, he informs me that there is only one route and to get back I would need to just reverse all the way I came up!

Remember, it's an eighteen-wheeler truck and even though I have four helpers, reversing downhill all the way is something I had never bargained for... but literally, there was no way out! I got on to the truck, asked my helpers to watch the sides, said a small prayer, shifted to reverse gear and slowly started my way down. Luckily, since it was the only house on top of the mountain, we were able to block any vehicle that was coming up and heart in my mouth, I moved on. The ordeal lasted for about three hours and at the end of it, I was extremely tired and felt exhausted. Another hurdle and another stepping stone...

I continue doing moves and am also concentrating on the further growth of the company and as such, don't notice a change in Joy's behaviour. It is only sometime in mid-January that I get to know that Joy has been speaking behind my back and complaining about me to Gidon. He has been telling Gidon that I give him credit only for the smaller jobs and that I am trying to hog the limelight by keeping all the bigger jobs. I also get to know that whenever I am out of the office Joy spends a lot of time in Gidon's cabin and I am the subject of discussion. I do not find any change in Gidon's behaviour towards me and so, decide to wait and watch before jumping to any conclusions. I also tell myself that it would be very difficult for someone to get Gidon to change his opinion about me.

Gidon and Shula continue to be very nice to me and at least thrice a week, Gidon and I have lunch together. On such occasions, in addition to talking about the office, we also talk about life in general, about the customs and traditions of Israel and so on. I learn from him that Tel Aviv and Jerusalem are important cultural hubs in Israel, the former being among the top ten cities for nightlife. I also get to learn a lot about Jerusalem and am also told that Israel has over 150 museums. More than once, over lunch, he has invited me to be his guest and visit Israel. I have always found Gidon a very interesting person to talk with and he has this ability to hold one's attention and motivate anyone who speaks with him.

17

Betrayal, One of Life's most Valuable Lessons

Anand, in the meanwhile, has moved on to his next job in an architect's office and begins to use the care more often. Gidon has obviously noticed this and in February, offers to lend me his Mercedes car on a very low monthly rental. I gladly accept and thank him for this gesture. This sets me thinking as to whether all my assumptions about Joy were unfounded because I knew Gidon would not be lending me his car if he was beginning to lose trust in me. This thought set my mind at ease and I continued doing my best with renewed vigour.

A month later, I decide to shift to a bigger place and find an apartment on Mansion Park Drive in Santa Clara. Anand does not move in with me since he decides to reside in Dublin, Ohio. The apartment with a patio has one bedroom and one hall which I use as the living –cum-dining room. I also make provision for a small puja enclosure in the hall.

When I see the calendar on the first of April, the red marking I have made against 17th April reminds me of the BMW and on 15th Anand and I drive down to the showroom in our Galant and meet Wahab. He confirms that I now qualify for the car loan and puts me on to the concerned sales person, who shows me the models on display and explains the costing and features. I choose a red colour vehicle and soon the paper work is complete. We are told that we would not need to exchange the Galant and as such, decide to keep this car so that Anand can continue to use it.

As I take delivery of the BMW and drive home, I feel top of the world owning my first new car in the US. The car's engine is powerful, sound system is great and I am especially impressed with the extended seats and climate package. As soon as I reach home, I call mom and give her the good news and she says, "Take care because a lot of people could get jealous and cast an evil eye on you... don't forget to pray before taking out the car... I too will do an *archanai* in your name."

A few days after I get the BMW, Gidon throws a party on the occasion of Shula having conceived their first baby. At the party, I stand up and folding my hands and closing my eyes, say a small prayer - *Mathru boodeshwara devo, Bakthanaam ishta thayaka, Sukanthi kunthala naavaha, Sukha Prasava Mrichchathuhuhu* – wishing her a safe delivery and when I explain the meaning, both, Gidon and Shula get emotional and thank me profusely. There's music, there's good food and of course, there's good wine too. The party goes on late into the night and all of us are too tired to attend office the next day.

At the office, Joy doesn't seem to be getting anywhere but quite often I notice that he and Gidon speak to each other in the Hebrew language when I am around and this gives me a vague feeling that I am the subject of their discussion and what is being discussed is not complimentary to me. However, I can see that Gidon does not seem to be in agreement with whatever Roy is telling him and this gives me some satisfaction.

In June, my younger brother Aditya and sister, Deepika visit us and since I now stay in a bigger apartment, they are comfortably accommodated. Anand too decides to stay at my place till they are there. We all spend a lot of time together, travel a bit, dine out and I do everything I can to make them feel happy. One evening, while we are together, we talk about Mom's birthday in August and I decide and announce that I am going to gift her car in Chennai. Both of them spend about ten days with Anand and me and then, leave for India.

I continue to do moves and the trip I make in July 2005 is something that I will never forget in my life. As I am almost half way through my journey, I am caught in a hurricane – Hurricane Cindy – and strong winds and heavy rain make driving very difficult. Fortunately, during my training at the driving school, I was given a few tips on driving under such vulnerable conditions and the three important tips I remembered were that one needs to look out for wires that have been knocked down and are dangling due to the storm, that one needs to maintain more distance than one normally does and very importantly, that one has to avoid sudden braking or turning the steering wheel until traction is regained.

As days pass by, I began to realise that Mom's guess about people getting jealous about me was right. Even though everyone knew that I had come up the hard way and through sheer determination and hard work, the very thought of my being successful was a cause of envy for some of them. The Tamil saying that people throw stones only at fruit bearing trees came to my mind but for me, even this was a learning experience as I got to know who my true friends were. I also got to learn that people are jealous because they think I have got something they want.

I also have this strange foreboding that I am going to land in trouble because of Joy but I also know that not one person in the organisation can point fingers at me an accuse me of being disloyal to the organisation. I also know that since Gidon considers me a big asset to the company, he would not do anything that could hurt or upset me. Let's wait and see, I tell myself again. In the meantime, I continue to call up and speak to my Mom and sister to keep them updated and whenever I do so, Mom keeps telling me to take care since jealousy can result in a lot of harmful energy being generated, and this could affect me. I assure her that I will take care and also tell her that the funds for the new car, my birthday gift, had already been transferred and that she could take delivery of the car on her birthday.

On September 11th, it's late in the night when I return from a trip and by the time I complete the log book and am finished for the day I see that the time is 3 a.m. on 12th, Just then I remember that 11th was the last date to make payments against my credit cards and as such, I go to my room in the office, start up the computer and get working on the online payments to be made. As I am doing so, I notice that Joy's wife walks in, glances at the computer screen to see what I am doing and, without a word, walks off. I begin to wonder as to what had kept her awake so long and also whether she walked in to the room with a specific purpose. I completed what I was doing and left.

The next day morning, which is the 12th of September, as soon as I enter the office, Gidon calls me on the phone and the first think he asks me is "Why were you doing your personal work on the office computer last night...?" I am shocked... I am dumbstruck! I quickly regain my composure and tell Gidon "It's because I have been working so hard for your company and have hardly found time to do my personal work... and, after all it was at 3 a.m. and not during office hours!" And without giving him a chance to interrupt, I continue, "However, now that you have chosen to cast an aspersion against me, I would like to quit... but no, I am not going to just walk out on you, I am giving you a thirty-day notice period effective today..."

At home that night, I begin to think of how much I had done for the company... of how affectionate Gidon and Shula had been... of all the good times we had and the more I thought about it, the more difficult it was to digest that Gidon had behaved this way. Obviously, Joy had brainwashed him and led him to believe that since the company had grown, they no longer needed my services. I call up Mom and tell her what happened and she says "you're not an amateur... you have proved your capabilities and the whole moving industry there knows... now it's your choice... choose what you want to do, and go ahead and do it... you just can't fail." Her words are very comforting and I decide to keep all my options open.

Over the next few days, Gidon behaves like nothing has happened and he tries to make me feel comfortable, possibly hoping that I would change my decision. By the 15th, he realises that I will not be changing my decision, and invites me to join him for a cup of coffee at Starbucks. As we are sipping our drink, Gidon asks me, "What are you planning to do?" and I reply, "Frankly, I just don't know but one thing's for sure... I am not working for you anymore."

Gidon nods and stays silent for about ten seconds, and then goes on "You know what... there was this guy who was workings for a company dealing in wood... after a couple of years, he left the company and started on his own but just two years after he started, he was found hanging from the ceiling of his shop..." I watch him as he continues, "You know, I am not trying to frighten or discourage you but there's a lot of black magic that could harm you..." This time however, his words do not impress me and I tell him that I just don't care and that I will choose whichever option is right for me.

18

I am the Boss...

A few days after I decide to resign, we are informed that the Public Utilities Commission intends to hold an audit of our records during the third week and since I represent the company at the PUC, I would need to handle it. Gidon calls me over and tells me that if I ensured a clean audit without any fines, he would pay me three thousand dollars as bonus. I tell him that I am not fascinated by his offer but will do my job and take care of the audit. The PUC conducts the audit and there are no fines. In the meantime, I hand over all the books and records to Gidon and Shula.

On the 9th of October, three days before I am scheduled to leave, Gidon calls me up as soon as I come in to the office and tells me that I am relieved with immediate effect and I can leave. I walk down to his room and ask him about my salary as well as the bonus of three thousand dollars and he assures me that he will pay me in two weeks. I bid goodbye to Shula and when the rest of the staff get to know that I am leaving, they all become emotional and each of them tells me how much they have learnt from me and the positive impact that I have had on their lives. I got to know that the staff had planned a party for me on the 11th and as they had not anticipated that I would leave earlier, they were not prepared... I realise how much they all love me and I am moved. They wish me good luck, ask me to stay connected and promise me that they will announce a party very soon.

As I walk out of the office and go past the trucks that are parked outside, my emotions get the better of me and I wipe the tears from my face. Another lesson learnt. My mom's words come to my mind and I feel reassured. When I go to bed, as I keep thinking on my future course of action, I remember the options Nadav had mentioned at his send-off party and wonder which option I should choose. I decide to sleep over it and it takes me quite a while to fall asleep

I wake up early on 10th October and after a bath, chant the Hanuman Chalisa hymn. I pray God to guide me and I also invoke Mom's blessings to begin a new phase in my life. After breakfast, I switch on the computer and as I glance through the news online, I see a headline which reads 'The right moment for start-up companies' and as I read through the article, my mind has been made up... I decide to start my own moving company and begin operations from my apartment in Santa Clara. I thank God for answering my prayers and am convinced that I have taken the right decision.

The moment I take a decision to start a company, I become very clear in my mind as to what my action plan will be. I first concentrate on applying for licenses – local and long distance. For long distance, the Department of Transportation is the licensing authority and for local moves, the Public Utilities Commission has to issue the license. The DOT issues the license in just two days and thanks to my already being a PUC certified mover, we will be getting the local moves license in thirty days after completing a few basic formalities. I then speak to the truck rental companies and since they already know my track record, assure me of their full support as well the best rates.

At this point of time I have two credit cards with which I am permitted a withdrawal of just 7500 dollars. However, this is not a deterrent to my efforts and I am confident that if I plan my expenses carefully, this money is sufficient to see me through till the revenues start coming in. My first task is to buy leads from Lead Generating Companies and I ask for two hundred leads. Six telephones and two insurance policies – one for the cargo and the other for the vehicle - are next on my expense list. I also appoint one driver. Now, I am all set to begin.

As I get down to work and begin to convert the leads into moves, I decide to appoint Parvathi whom I had got to know through one of the social networking websites, to help me out in sales, and I consider myself lucky to have her with me because she is to me what I was to Gidon. She works extra hours, gives her all for the company and her objective is to make our company the number one in the industry. Her ability to respond immediately to leads received ensures a very high rate of conversion and the orders start increasing.

Sam whom I have known since my days with Gidon, offers to help out and I take him in as a Foreman. He works for me free for a few days and I am so impressed with his work that when he suggests that I make him a partner, and also agrees to invest twenty thousand dollars in the company sometime in January, I take him on board. I decide that he will oversee Operations and I, Sales and Customer Care. I have two big boards put up and these boards are used to display sales targets, truck movements, performance figures, future projections etc. This is done more to motivate the staff and get them to witness the growth of the company. Everyday morning from 8 to 8.30, Parvathi and I have a meeting and we discuss the figures on the boards. Business is gradually picking up and the money starts coming in.

On the 25th of October I visit Brunocorp and after clearing all the accounts with Shula, walk up to Gidon and ask him for the three thousand plus dollars that I have to get paid. He just puts on a straight fact and simply tells me that he cannot pay me, and that I was free to do whatever I want! He seemed to be a totally different person now and I just couldn't believe it. I hide my feelings of surprise and shock and with a smile ask him "how many orders do you have this month?" "Seventy," he replies. With a look of seriousness on my face and a tone of authority in my voice, I tell him, "Gidon, you know how I'm going to repay you for what you've done to me... next month, I will see to it that I get at least one order more than what you have and after that, you'll see who has the last laugh," and I storm out of his cabin. As soon as I go back to my office, the first thing I do is, change the password to *b-1up-ongidon.*

During November, after completion of thirty days, I take stock of the position and am convinced that we are on the growth path... the revenue inflow also confirms this. I now decide to order our first new vehicle, a 26' box truck from Oakland and arrange for the chassis to be fabricated and mounted as per our specifications. I also arrange to get a logo of our company ready and get it painted on the truck. Now, our first new truck is ready to roll!

It has always been my firm belief that if one works hard and earns well, he also needs to spend well on himself and his family, get out and have fun because if you concentrate only on work and you do not enjoy life, you will always be under pressure and miss out on all the good things in life. This may sound amusing but I am almost certain that how much you earn is directly proportionate to how much you spend enjoying life... the more you spend, the more you earn, and I think this is true not just about money but about most things in life.

In October, my sister Deepika visits me and as usual brings a lot of home cooked goodies to eat. Whenever she visits us, which is at least once in six months, the three of us – Anand, Deepika and I – paint the town red. This time, I decide that I will not cut corners on expenditure and I spend well to ensure that she enjoys herself and the three of us have a great time. We visit entertainment parks, dine out at the best restaurants, splurge on ice creams and chocolates... and before we even realise it, my sister has to fly back to India. However, before she leaves, she gives me just one piece of sisterly advice... she says "Anna, I did not tell you this before but I really felt scared at the speed in which you were driving the BMW...I know the roads tempt you but... well, please be careful..., and the look in her eyes and tone of her voice conveyed her concern for me. I promised her that I would be careful.

19

Sunnyvale it is, and then it's off to Pismo Beach

Towards the end of November, when I see that the revenue inflow is good, I decide to indulge in a new car and immediately the Ferrari comes to my mind. It was sometime in April last year that I had spoken to Nadav on the subject and at that point of time, I had given myself two years to own a Ferrari... I still had six months left. I think about it... to buy or not to buy... think of Mom's advice telling me not to let success go to my head and then decide that I should not be splurging on a Ferrari at this point in my life... it could even make me feel guilty. I would rather go slow and wait for some more time but I am determined that I would get it one day within the deadline.

My next choice is the BMW 7 Series. I visit the same showroom from where I bought my BMW 5 Series car. As luck would have it, they have an exclusive fully loaded 2006 deep green metallic BMW 7 Series 750li... it's a beauty and I go for it. It takes some time for the salesman to explain all the features of the car and by the time he is done, I am desperate to get behind the wheel. The car comes with the versatile idrive consisting of an LCD panel which is mounted in the dashboard along with a control knob positioned on the centre console. The idrive is used for operating the television, DVD, cruise control, infrared night vision etc. The car has a great throttle response too and is a pleasure to drive.

I call up Mom and my sister and update them on the progress I am making as well as the new car and they assure me that I have taken the right decision in starting a company. Mom's only piece of advice is "Remember everything that I have told you... and whatever success and fame that you may achieve, never ever let it go to your head... as long as you have your feet firmly on the ground, you will continue to rise higher and higher and let the world know that you are an entity which is not bound to any limits." Mom always seemed to have the right advice for me and I am happy that I have not broken the New Year resolution I had made.

Towards the end of November I got one more credit card and since I had chosen to put off buying a Ferrari, I thought I was justified in wanting to own the two wheeler I had always longed for – the Kawasaki Ninja 600. Immediately after Uncle had stopped allowing me to ride his bike, I had visited the Kawasaki showroom only to be told that I did not qualify for a loan, and ever since, I had wanted to own a bike. Now, I just walked into the showroom, paid up in full and rode out with my dream bike.

On Saturday mornings I zoom around on my Kawasaki and enjoy fun rides on the 56-kilometre California State Route 9 that passes through the scenic rural and wooded San Lorenzo Valley and the Saratoga Gap. I also make it a point to attend the Bike Meets that are held at 11 a.m. on every Saturday morning at the Blue Coast Coffee Shop on Route 9. This is another good learning experience for me because at such meets, I get to meet a lot of bike enthusiasts as well as professional racers and discuss various issues related to bikes and cars. Through the meets, I also keep track of all the forthcoming car and bike launches, and also get to know about other automobile related events.

As the CEO of my company, I get to interact with a lot of high profile individuals and now, I can see that my new car reflects my status in society. Whenever I drive down to business or luncheon meetings, I can notice the difference in the way I am received and treated by some of the doyens in the industry and society. Suddenly I find that clinching large business deals and moving up in society is getting easier. Even my colleagues and friends are convinced that I had arrived and they begin treating me with awe and respect... it's an odd feeling but I guess that's what fame and success is about.

In December we have a quarterly review meeting and I find the progress satisfactory... in fact, I observe that we could do much better if we increased our vehicle and staff strength. After the meeting, I once again personally reconfirm the financial status of the company and after considering all the pros and cons, decide to go in for a small expansion.

I get in touch with a truck company in Oakland and speak to Joel Neithen, a good friend of mine. Conscious of the fact that I need to watch every step that I take, I decide against going in for a new truck and Joel helps me find a used truck. The down payment is a little high but I think it is worth it and decide to take it.

Next on my expansion plan is the recruitment of sales personnel and I hire Darren who proves to be a very good performer. Darren and Parvathi make a great team and as I begin to buy more leads, the number of conversions too is increasing. Everything seems set but internal communication between departments is a problem and now it becomes obvious that I have to shift the office to a bigger place so that all of us can operate comfortably from a single location and we can also be prepared for further expansion whenever required.

Fortunately, I am able to find an office space in Sunnyvale but before I shift, there is one issue I need to resolve: the lease agreement for the present office in Santa Clara is up to June 2006 and we are now in December 2005... we still have six months left. If we shift before the lease period, we are liable to pay rent up to the lease period and this would be a great loss! As I begin to try and find a solution, I get to learn that the demand for space in Santa Clara is very high and as such, the leasing and rental costs too have gone up. Taking advantage of the situation, I release an ad and within no time, find an occupant. After paying up the processing fee and completing a few formalities, the new occupant is ready to move in. It looks like things are continuing to work out well for me and luck and destiny are complementing each and every action of mine.

Sometime in mid-December, with the team in place, office set and business on the upswing, Sam and I feel like taking a small break and we go to Pismo Beach in the Central Coast area of California. It's a ninety minute drive from our place and while I take my car, Sam prefers to ride his bike since he likes to show off all his acrobatic riding skills on such trips. He is capable of riding long distances on just one of the two wheels with the other wheel elevated and it's a thrill to watch him performing such stunts. At Pismo Beach, for the first time in my life, I get to see sand dunes and ride a Quad bike which is a 4-wheeler All-terrain vehicle (ATV). Sam and I also do some wind surfing and canoeing and we go all out to enjoy ourselves, and yes, we do not cut corners as far as the spending is concerned.

This New Year in 2006, I decide to stay put in California, and throw a party for all my staff. I spend enough money to make the occasion very special and also make my staff feel very comfortable so that they appreciate that I would like to share the good times too with all of them. At the party I express my gratitude to each one of them for their contribution and also give them a small memento on the occasion. I also arrange for some fun filled events and at the stroke of 12 midnight, in a surprise move, with music in the background, they unfurl a velvet banner which reads "Thank you boss... we love you and we'll be with you." I had not expected this and I was moved beyond words.

During the second week of January, we move in to the Sunnyvale office and Sam and I decide to reside here too. Again, it looks like as if the office has been specially designed for me, and waiting for me to move in. Covering an area of about four thousand square feet, it has six rooms in the ground floor, and two small rooms and one big room upstairs... just like I had wanted, enough space for all the staff to work comfortably, and for further expansion too. Luck continues to favour me and I am also able to locate warehouses close by as well as get space for parking the trucks. Now, all of us operate from one office and the trucks are parked in the self-storage parking lot also used to store customers' goods.

20

Setting Foot in Los Angeles

Immediately after we move in to the new office, Kalai calls and asks me if she can join me. I have always seen that whenever one leaves and starts on his own, he always attempts to woo all the star performers of the old company to his company but in my case, star performers of Brunocorp seemed to be keen on joining me. I ask Kalai to join and my team seems to be almost complete.

A few days after Kalai joines, Vidya, a Chartered Accountant and one more star performer of Brunocorp is keen on joining me and I take her in to handle all the accounts work. Now the allocation of responsibilities is also done and everyone has a specific responsibility – Sam handles Operations, Parvathi, Darren and Kalai handle sales and customer service, Vidya handles the accounts and I oversee the entire operations and also step in whenever needed to handle a particular situation in any of the departments.

Of course, like any other office, all is not smooth and sometimes there is conflict of interest among staff and as the CEO, I do everything possible to douse the flames before they turn into a raging fire. When I find that Parvathi and Kalai do not seem to get along well, I shift Parvathi to Customer Relations and follow-up and convince her that this is being done to prepare her for bigger responsibilities.

Three months into running the company, like any other start-up company, we too have our hiccups and sometimes find it difficult to manage the necessary funds to either pay our suppliers or meet other expenses but luckily, we have comfortably got out of such situations by tactful management of funds and identifying the vulnerable areas of operation.

I realise that there are quite a few factors that have a negative impact on the inflow of funds and servicing a bad customer is one of them. There are customers who do not have the inclination to pay and end up paying only for part of the services. For example, if the job takes six hours, they are willing to pay only for three hours and want the balance amount waived. There are also customers who agree to pay for part services but end up paying nothing! Then, there are customers who do not understand that our contract stipulates payment for a minimum duration of three hours and if the job gets over in two hours, are willing to pay only for this. When it comes to packing of the goods, some customers are unwilling to pay packing charges and even if the subsequently agree to pay, bargain for the lowest rates.

As the business keeps growing, I try to identify all the issues that are having a negative impact on our business and one by one, through trial and error, find ways to correct the system wherever required. I notice that when one issue is solved, there's always another issue crying for attention. I concentrate on proper structuring of the operations and I do this in a phased manner, knowing fully well that this is going to be a continuous process.

In addition to buying leads from lead generating companies, I also aim at getting in more orders directly and look at the options available. I check with some of my contacts in senior positions and many of them suggest that I try out the Yellow Pages. Since the company is doing well and we can now afford an ad spend, I decide to go ahead and ask my Sales team to collect the advertisement rates, circulation figures, areas of distribution and other details of Yellow Pages. I also make provision for a tentative ad budget for the next six months. I am now all set to reach out to more customers.

Before planning my ad schedule in Yellow Pages, in order to choose the right editions, I check out the demographic details on the internet and I learn that there are fifty six counties in California, and I decide to release ads in the relevant editions to reach all the counties. As I am browsing the net and checking out the details, purely by chance, I also discover that there is great potential for our business in Los Angeles and many of the customers there are looking for reputed service oriented moving companies located in their neighbourhood. It was as if some unknown force was showing me the way to take my company to the next level... it was as if I just had to think about my next move and the doors showing me how to go about it would automatically open.

In early February, after finding a suitable place, I open up a branch office in Los Angeles and send two helpers and two movers to operate from there. Since I am already familiar with all the formalities and since all our business associates also have their offices in LA, operations are on stream right from day one. I also get a phone connection with the local three-digit code number because even though there is no difference in call rates between a local number and an outstation number, I know that customers feel more comfortable in dealing with a neighbourhood company that is easily accessible to them.

I have always believed that to run any successful business, one needs to take the staff into confidence and seek their inputs on issues that are relevant to the company's progress. I am also aware that some of the best ideas that have led to the success of many companies have emanated not from the top level but from the middle and lower level personnel. As such, in my company too, weekend luncheon barbeques are arranged for all the staff on Fridays and in an informal way, issues relating to the progress of the company are discussed, and suggestions for improvement sought from all the personnel immaterial of their position in the company.

With both the offices doing very well, the bottom line too keeps getting better, and as is my policy, I decide to spend on a new wardrobe, a bigger television and a few more luxuries. I also begin to party more often with Sam and some of my other friends and business contacts. JJ's Blues on Stevens Creek Boulevard in San Jose is one of our favourite and regular haunts and I just love the music and ambience. I love Italian food and Acquerello, La Ciccia and Da Flora are some of restaurants I frequent at Bay Area. However, I take care to ensure that I do not go overboard and be extravagant, and I also make sure that all my staff too has nothing to complain about.

As days pass by, I start getting a lot of negative feedback about Sam from my colleagues like Parvathi and Kalai as well as from some of my well-wishers like Nadav. They try to warn me about Sam and tell me that he always has an ulterior motive for doing something, and that, since I hold all responsibility for the assets of the company even though he too is a partner, I need to be cautious in my dealings with him. Even though I respect everyone's concern, it does not worry me much since I am open to learn from mistakes and willing to pay the price.

I am prepared to face any kind of experience, good or bad, and also prepared to lose in order to gain... what I could lose by way of money would be a miniscule of what I would gain or learn by the experience. I also strongly believe that if I shirk bad experiences at this stage in my life, I will never learn to face up to similar experiences ever in my life. As such, i ignore all the warnings about Sam and put them out of my mind

I call up my Mom and sister and share details about the company's progress with them and I also tell them that now, I can at least think about owning all the luxuries in life. Mom is happy for me and also advises me to ensure that as much as I spend on myself, I should also keep others in mind and help out the needy, whoever it be. She also tells me that at no point of time should I ever forget that I have my roots in India and as such, giving back to the motherland must also be part of my agenda. Frankly, I had not thought of this aspect but now, store the thought in my mind and save it for future reference and action. Mom also informs me that Deepika, my sister, had shared her concerns about my driving at high speeds and I assure her that I will take care.

21

The Bottom Line is Good and it's Time for the Ferrari

Towards the middle of February, Sam approaches me and suggests that I sell my bike, the Kawasaki Ninja 600, and get myself the latest version. He offers to sell it for me and I sign the papers and give it to him. At about the same time, since more funds are required for further expansion of the company, I tell Sam to bring in his investment of twenty thousand dollars and he promises to do so in the next few days. In about a week's time, Sam deposits twenty thousand dollars in the company's bank account and tells me that this is towards his share of the investment in the company. I am happy that he has kept his word and plan out the expenditure for our next expansion programme.

A few days later I ask Sam about the bike and he tells me that the deal would get over soon. However, to my shock and surprise, I get to know that the twenty thousand dollars which Sam had deposited as his share of the investment in the company was in fact, the sale proceeds of my Kawasaki bike! This is yet another learning experience for me and I don't mind the price I am paying for it. I also believe that everything happens for a reason and no one really is a bad person... it is only that the person tends to overlook or miss the thin line between good and bad and in the process, hurts others. If we can help the person see that thin line and help him avoid overstepping it, then we would have fewer "bad" people in the world, and pain and sorrow would be reduced to a great extent.

Things are going well but the fact that restructuring and streamlining the operations of a company is a continuous process is proved once again when, one day in May, Kalai walks up to me and tells me that she has an offer from Shuki and the package is much better. I knew this was coming since I had noticed of late that she was not interacting with Parvathi and Sam like she used to. She also had a few personal issues but on more than one occasion I had very clearly told her that such issues should not be affecting her official work. I am sure that it would not make sense to keep her any longer and as such, tell her that since I would not be able to match Shuki's offer she is welcome to leave any time she wishes to.

On the day she leaves, Kalai comes in to my room and tells me how grateful she is to me for having given her the opportunity to work for the company and how good a mentor I have been...I wish her luck and she promises to stay in touch and leaves.

In May, six months after having stared the company, I call for a meeting with all senior personnel of the company and have a half-yearly review meeting. The Operations team, the Sales team and representatives of the LA office explain the progress they have been making, through power point presentations and as I see the facts and figures unfolding, I feel proud that I am now a successful entrepreneur, am a force to reckon with in the moving industry and also am now one among the upper echelons of the business world... I have kept my promise to Mom and she ought to be very pleased with my progress since I left India.

After the review meeting, I also have a one-to-one meeting with Vidya to reconfirm the financial status of the company and she assures me that the bottom line is quite healthy and the future prospects are good. In the night I go out for dinner and am all by myself. As I wait for food to be served, I think about my present status... a successful entrepreneur, financially sound and the business strategically poised for sustained growth... well, what else can I ask for? Dinner is served and I am reminded of Mom's words... I should not allow success to go into my head... because after all, I am still far away from the pinnacle of success and as Robert Frost wrote, have many more promises to keep and miles to go before I sleep.

Just as I finish dinner, I ask myself what next...maybe open up more offices... get into an alliance with other international moving companies... aim to be among the Fortune 500 companies... get written about in the Forbes magazine...? Oh yes, why not? But before that, I would like to keep one promise I made to myself and that is, to own my dream car... to own a Ferrari. Yes, indeed, I am going to own a Ferrari!

Just as things are settling down, in the last week of July, Sam's behaviour leads to an unpleasant incident. On a Tuesday morning, he notices that someone is trying to tow away our truck from where it has been parked. He accosts the tow truck driver and after an argument, hits him and leaves him bleeding. When the cops arrive, Sam is nowhere to be found and soon the cops are at my office. I assure the cops that I will get Sam to surrender and ask Sam to report to the police immediately which he does. As a result of this incident, the Storage Units Manager gives us an eviction notice.

Fortunately, again luck favours me and I am able to find a 25000 square feet warehouse situated just behind Gidon's office... I pay the advance and sign the lease agreement on August 1st. Now, I have enough space to park six or seven trucks and provision to park another twenty or thirty trucks.

Mom is scheduled to visit me in August and will be spending her birthday in the US. On her last birthday I had gifted a car and I was wondering what I ought to do this year to make her happy. Suddenly it dawns on me that for any mother, her children's happiness is what matters most and when she sees her children are happy, she is overjoyed and her happiness peaks. Further, even from my school days, I have noticed that whenever I have had to take crucial decisions and sought Mom's advice, she has felt very happy about it and takes great satisfaction in offering me her counsel.

As such, even though I have made up my mind and am inclined to buy a Ferrari, I feel that seeking Mom's opinion on the subject would not only make me feel more confident but would also make her feel happy. What's more, if I could take delivery of the car on her birthday, then that would be her happiest moment. In the meantime, I decide to check out the used car showrooms and am greatly impressed with a Ferrari 360 Modena 2004 on display at a particular outlet. I decide that this is going to be my car.

Mom arrives during the second week of August and as usual, Anand too comes over to stay with me while she is here. The day she comes, in the night, as we are having dinner together, I tell Mom about my desire to own a Ferrari and ask her what she thinks about it. She tells me, "I think it's a little too early to think about such an expensive car but since I am sure you are going to only get better and better and it's going to be sooner or later, if owning a Ferrari now will make you happy, go ahead." Immediately after Mom approves, I contact the showroom, confirm the purchase, and arrange for the other formalities to be completed. The down payment is made and my Ferrari Modena is ready.

It is 11th August and I choose to take to take delivery of the car on my Mom's birthday, the 14th of August. However, I am told that this is not possible since the insurance policy specific to a Ferrari would take more than the time normally taken for other cars. I then explain the significance of 14th August and after also speaking to a few senior people, they agree for delivery on 14th August.

22

The Ferrari Arrives but is the Road ahead Clear?

It's 14th August and I wish Mom a very happy birthday. She leaves for the Shiv Durga temple at about 7 a.m. and I take the day off to be with her. In the afternoon we have a home cooked lunch that includes *payasam* and my Mom's favourite sweet, the *Rasamalai* which I order from the Bikaner Sweets and Chaat Café in Sunnyvale. In the evening we go to take delivery of the Ferrari. Even though it's a 2004 model used car, it looks like new and I am eager to get behind the wheel. The sales personnel ask us to wait till they get the papers ready and I ask Mom to relax in the lounge.

While I am waiting for the papers to get ready, I move around the showroom and a classy Bugatti Veyron EB 164 catches my eye. With a top speed of 407 kilometres per hour, it is probably the fastest car in the world. Normally one is not permitted to open or even touch such cars displayed in the showrooms but since I had confirmed the purchase of the Ferrari and nobody would mind, I get in to the car for just the feel... it is fabulous! I get out of the car and notice that it has a very low ground clearance space, probably less than 5 inches!

The papers are ready and I walk over to where the Ferrari is parked. It's a two-seater sports coupe with a V8 engine and it is lightweight but very powerful. The sales person explains the basic features of the car – the gear operations, the driver seat manually adjustable lumbar support, the climate control, the sound system with six total speakers and two subwoofers and lots more... it's a dream car. I ask him what the top speed is and he says that it is 295 kilometres per hour and also tells me that the 1-100 acceleration speed takes just 4.3 seconds.

We both then go on a test drive and I get to operate the paddle shift with the start-stop and reverse buttons. As we drive, I also listen to the loud bass rumble of the 2B exhaust and I just love it. What a piece of marvel! It's about 7.30 p.m. when I take delivery of the car and just before we leave, Mom and I close our eyes and say a small prayer. Mom again asks me to wait a little, checks out if the inauspicious time of the day is past, and then we leave and as we leave, I once again look at the Bugatti Veyron and tell myself that this is going to be my next car. We head for Chang's China Bistro Chinese restaurant for dinner and as I get a feel of the car, I make sure that I don't drive fast since Mom's with me.

At dinner, we discuss the new car and while explaining the features to her, I also mention that the top speed is 295 kilometres per hour. She suddenly looks concerned, drinks a little water and looking straight into my eyes says, "Deepu (Deepika) did mention to me that you drive rather fast... and now you are telling me that the top speed is 295... I am beginning to get a little worried... look, I want you to be very very careful when you drive and...," I cut her short and say "Mom, I'll be careful, don't worry" and holding her hands, tell her, "Thanks for all that you have done for me... I love you Mom!" She is scheduled to fly back to India tomorrow and after dinner we head for home.

As we are nearing home, I remember what I told Nadav about two years back. When Mom and I get home, I tell her that I will join her a little later and picking up my phone, call up Nadav and ask him to come over. I then park the Ferrari near the warehouse, walk down a short distance and wait for Nadav. It's about 10 p.m. when he comes and presuming that I had called him to discuss business asks me where I would prefer to go for dinner. I smile at him and say "Nadav, do you remember what I told you about two years back?" Again, he thinks that I am talking about some business deal and he asks me if it's got something to do with one of the incidents while on a San Jose-New York trip. I smile again and tell him, "Remember what I told you while going by the Ferrari showroom... remember I told you that I would own a Ferrari in two years... and remember I promised you that I would let you know when I bought the car...?" Giving Nadav the keys and leading him to the car I go on, "Now, there's my Ferrari and here are the keys... go, take a drive and tell me how the car feels."

Nadav becomes emotional and giving me a big hug says, "You're amazing... oh my God, you've done it man...!" I choose to let Nadav experience the car all by himself and so I stay back and ask him to go ahead. Nadav gets in to the car, revs up the engine, zooms past me and disappears out of sight. I expect him back in about ten minutes but he returns after twenty minutes. As he gets out of the car and walks towards me, he lifts his hand, shows a thumbs up sign and says, "It's a fantastic car... congrats, best of luck and God bless!." He then looks at me and says, "And man, it was so nice of you to have remembered me and offered me a drive... I'll never forget this." He goes on and asks, "Tell me something... is everyone in India as nice and likeable as you are... what a great country!" I just tell him, "Why not visit India and check it out for yourself... I'll be your host?" Nadav and I kept talking about old times and it's close to midnight when he leaves.

When I was quite young and first learnt riding a cycle, I remember that I always used to wait for one excuse or the other to just hop on to the cycle and ride away, and whenever I did so I always used to ride a little farther than necessary just for the fun of it. Today, with my Ferrari, I seem to be experiencing the same feel and excitement, and am eager to take the car and just drive, even if it is to the coffee shop that's just down the road. Now, however, I also begin to experience something more – as I drive, it looks like the whole world is watching me and it feels like I have suddenly been upgraded to VIP status. Again, I remember my mom's words and tell myself that I am just imagining things and I still have a lot to learn and a long way to go.

Whenever I drive down to Starbucks, I also get friendly with some of the cops who have come in for a cup of coffee, and can see that they too are very impressed with my Ferrari. I encourage them to get in to the car and let them look at the controls and the engine as well as listen to the effects of the sound system. They appreciate my gesture and when I am leaving they even help me back up and with a smile on their faces, bid goodbye.

One evening, as I am driving back home, I feel the car wobbling a little and suspect that this is due to low tyre pressure in one of the back tyres. As I cruise along, a bit cautious, I notice a yellow Ferrari parked very near my home and hoping that I would be able to get some help, park my car and walk over to meet the owner of the parked vehicle. His name is Khalil and when I tell him about the low tyre pressure, he manages to locate a tyre pressure gauge and does the needful. He goes on to tell me that he has set up a tyre shop at the spot and will be opening tomorrow.

As we get talking, he also tells me that he has heard about me from some of his contacts in the moving industry as well as some of his friends who visit Starbucks regularly. He also invites me to be present for the inauguration of his shop. Something tells me that destiny has planned this meeting with Khalil and there is a purpose to it.

The news of my buying a Ferrari seems to have spread among the bigwigs of the industry and in addition to my business contacts calling and congratulating me, even a few unknown industry people call up. I get a lot of new friends and since having bought the Ferrari, I note that my network of friends has increased by about twenty per cent but of course, I am conscious of the fact that many of them could be fair-weather friends.

23

Temptations Accost more often than Opportunities Knock

Sometime during end of August, I get a call from Rami , a business contact and good friend of mine who works for another moving company, and he invites me to join him on a four-day all-expense paid weekend fun trip to Lake Tahoe from 1st to 4th September which are holidays. Lake Tahoe is a freshwater lake at a surface elevation of 6225 feet, along the border between California and Nevada. We both decide to go by Rami's vehicle which is a Hummer and Rami decides to tow his boat with the car. Lake Tahoe is a five-hour drive from Sunnyvale.

From the time we reach Lake Tahoe, it is fun and only fun all the way. We visit the Pope Beach with its dunes and pine trees and go for some boating and cycling. Incidentally, this beach is in no way connected to the head of the Roman Catholic Church, and is named after the George Pope family which had built several summer estates in the 19th century. This totally unspoiled beach also offers a breath-taking view of the majestic Mount Tallac with a 9739 feet elevation.

Rami and I also ride a high speed gondola to the top of Heavenly Mountain and the view from the first observation point is fantastic. There is a restaurant serving food and drinks at the highest point and those who do not ski can simply sit on the benches laid out and just enjoy the sight of the snowy mountain. We also visit the Lower Eagle Falls which offers a spectacular view of the lake and Emerald Bay.

In addition to visiting a few more tourist spots, we also do a lot of trekking and swimming and when we are tired out and want to just relax, we opt for the Trout Farm where we try our hand at fishing and even manage to get some fish. The owner of the farm offers to clean the fish for us and in the night, we barbecue our catch and relish the tastiest trout we have eaten in years. At Lake Tahoe there are a lot of spots where one can just relax, swim or have a barbecue.

I have always wanted to do a balloon ride and at Lake Tahoe I get the opportunity. Early in the morning at about 7 a.m., after registration, we are taken to the boat and get introduced to the crew before the launch. Pastries, pies and fruit juice are available before the launch and at the given time, the balloon is launched from the boat... up, up and up we go and as we get higher and higher, the views over Lake Tahoe are a fantastic sight to watch. The balloon ride lasts for about ninety minutes and then it's a perfect landing on the boat... wow, what an experience!

On the last day of the trip Rami suggests that we try our luck at the Casino and I tell him that I'm game. I remember the time when Simbu and I visited a casino in London and how I was awed by the amount of money that was being bet at the tables and also by the whole atmosphere there. However, at that point of time we had not bet at the tables and had just observed the games and the players.

It's about 7.30 p.m. when we enter one of the casinos and Rami suggested that we play the Texas Holdum (also known as Texas hold'em). He explains to me that this is a variation of the standard game of poker where each player is dealt two cards face down and then, five community cards are dealt in three stages face-up and kept in front of the player. This game is a battle of wits and more than winning the game, a player tries to psychologically influence decisions on how much to bet or call. An expert player is adept at enhancing the opponents betting and thereby maximizes his gain at every round.

I tell Rami that I am not interested in the specifications of the game and that I am playing only for the fun of it. I try to observe the actions and body language of other players to check out on whether a particular type of action or movement influences a win but there is absolutely no indication of this kind... everyone looks like he is playing in a very natural and routine manner and nobody gives away any clue or indication of their strategy. I tell Rami that I would like to observe for a little more time before I plunge into action and walk around the tables to observe the players but after I finish, I am no wiser than before.

What a contrast to my official interactions! At business meetings, within a short time of starting the discussions, I am normally able to gauge the other person's line of thought and respond and react in a way that is to my benefit and advantage... however, at the Casino I am totally blank! This is a learning experience for me and I realise that I need to go a long way in understanding human psychology.

Rami and I then choose a table and I place a bet of a hundred dollars on a game of Texas Holdum... and I lose! I am not disappointed because something tells me that I played a little too early for my luck to keep pace and the next game I would win. But this is a game and not business and so would luck still favour me...? I convince myself that luck cannot distinguish between work and fun and if I am destined to be lucky, lucky will I be. So I turn to Rami and since it's his party, he gives me three hundred dollars to spend and asks me to try again. I decide to bet just thirty dollars, say a small prayer and get going... the suspense builds up... will I?... wont I?... and oh my God!, I hit a Royal Flush which means an ace-high straight flush such as A K Q J 10! I am declared winner and pick up the prize money of 1500 dollars! I am surprised with myself but I know I can't take the credit... I can almost see Lady Luck giving me a small wink. I am tempted to go at it again but decide against it and we leave for Sunnyvale.

As soon as I reach home, I call Mom and tell her about my fun trip to Lake Tahoe and especially about winning 1500 dollars. Sounding very angry, she retorts, "You aren't spending time gambling and wasting all your hard earned money are you...?" I understand her concern and explain to her that it was just a one-off incident and that I did it just for fun and nothing else. It took quite some time explaining to her but at the end of the conversation she was convinced that I was speaking the truth and all she says is, "In life, temptation will try to accost you more often than opportunities will knock at your door... and you have to be discerning enough to seize only the opportunities and give temptation the go-by...." And to emphasize her point she adds, "It is easier to avoid temptation than to resist it... so, just avoid temptation and you'll observe that there are more opportunities coming your way."

As I go to sleep in the night, Mom's words weigh heavily on me and I realise that she now has two concerns about me – my driving with great speed and my ability to resist temptation. I also realize that her concerns are justified and decide to give it a lot of thought in the days to come.

During the first week of October, I call for a meeting to review the Q2 performance and am glad to note that the company is on course and has been doing as per projected targets. Vidya however cautions me that we ought not to get complacent, and that we could possibly increase the targets so that we can outperform competition and increase our market share to be on par with the top ten moving companies in the US. I fully agree and ask her to work out the figures and share it with me so that we can brief the staff and take it forward.

It's almost two months since I started driving the Ferrari and now I am fully familiar with the operations... I have also overcome the "I'm driving a new car" syndrome and feel completely at ease behind the wheel. The fact that I can do a top speed of 295 kilometres per hour keeps popping up and once in a way, I am tempted to open the throttle and zoom, but I remember Mom's concerns and check my speed. At the same time, I also tell myself that I need to attempt a test drive at least to find out and get to know how the car performs at high speeds rather than to demonstrate my driving skills. I decide to do this soon and can barely wait.

It's the second week of October and I get an idea... why not throw a party for all my staff on the occasion of the first anniversary of the company? They deserve it for having given their all for the company, and they also need to be convinced that the company cares for them and wants them to have fun once in a way after all the hard work they have put in...to celebrate life, and to enjoy themselves. I decide to have the party on 25th October at one of the best hotels in San Francisco and also invite the staff from our Los Angeles office as well. I inform all the staff and they feel very happy about it.

24

At 240, even Luck Gets Scared… Good Bye!

On the 19th of October, I receive an invite from the Ferrari dealer to attend the Monterey Sports Car Championships to be held on 21st October at the Laguna Seca Raceway (Laguna Seca is Spanish for "dry lake") at Monterey. The racetrack built in 1957 is so named because the area on which it now lies was once a lake. It is a very prestigious event and I feel lucky to have been invited. I am aware that the world's best car racers will be participating and driving some of the world's fastest cars.

At the Championship event, before the beginning of the race, I get to meet many car racing enthusiasts and also get to learn that the racetrack has a 180 feet elevation change as well as a challenging downhill plunging turn, popularly known as the 8 and 8A combination turn, which is considered to be one of the world's most difficult to manoeuvre. Various other turns on the track have been named after former Formula 1 World Champions or other very successful race winners.

At the event I also get to meet two very important and influential people. The first is a billionaire who owns many top end models of the Ferrari and he has come to the event in his Ferrari Enzo. Only 399 Enzos were manufactured for customers and the 400th and last car was offered as a gift to His Holiness Pope John Paul II. The billionaire appears to be a very modest person and talks to me about his passion for Ferraris, and also goes on to explain some of the very exclusive features of the models in his possession. He also invites me to visit him so that we can spend more time discussing cars and I can also see the entire range of his cars.

The second person I meet is Robert F. Martin, owner of one of the racing teams participating in the Championships. He is in his late sixties and I have already heard about him since I have been interacting with the truck leasing company he owns. I find him to be a very unassuming person and he is all excited about how his team is going to perform. I go on to tell him about my passion for cars and bikes and he very casually informs me that he was himself a wining racer in the 1950s. As we shake hands, he says, "I can see that you are very passionate about everything you do... mark my words, in a couple of years from now, you're going to make it big." I am awed and humbled by his modesty.

On 23rd October, two days after the Championship event, as I am speaking to the Ferrari dealer on the phone, I am informed by him that the billionaire whom I had met at the event, died after his Enzo crashed in to a tree on his way back home. Even though he had been driving at a slow speed, the car had skidded and crashed.

Wednesday, 25th October 2006. It's the day of the party and I decide that I am going to enjoy myself in the company of all my staff. Sam's friend, Wang Wei, a Chinese national is with us. It's about 7 p.m. and since I have booked the table at the San Francisco hotel for 11 p.m., we decide to spend about two hours at the JJ's Blues in San Jose. I ask Sam to drive my BMW and just as I get in to the Ferrari, Wang walks over to me and going around the car, keeps gazing at it... somehow, I am not happy with the way he is staring at the car. He asks if he can travel with me in the Ferrari and I ask him to get in. We drive down to JJ's Blues and the first phase of the party begins.

At about 10 p.m., we decide to leave San Jose and drive down to San Francisco, again, Sam in the BMW and Wang and myself in the Ferrari. It's a 75 kilometre drive and looking at Wang's face and listening to him speak, I can see that he is beginning to feel a little jealous about me... again I feel a little disturbed and uneasy. As we enter the hotel, the valet is waiting to park my car in the special guests' parking lot. Wang and I get out of the car and enter the foyer and Sam joins us in ten minutes. Our staff has been here since 8.30 p.m., and enjoying themselves with a lot of fun filled entertainment. As Sam, Wang and I enter, they welcome us with a big applause. I just ask them to keep enjoying themselves and feel happy for them.

The party goes on and as I continue to have a great time, I forget about everything else and just celebrate life and enjoy the moment. At about 3.15 a.m., we decide to leave and ask the valet to fetch our cars. Since Wang is not steady on his feet, I nudge him on to the seat of the Ferrari. And then, in a flash, I suddenly remember about the speed check I had wanted to do on the Ferrari. "Why not do the speed check now?" I ask myself. After all, at this hour, the roads would be free of traffic and I had decided to do a speed check anyway. Without any further thought, I decide that this is the right time to do it and the thrill and excitement builds up.

I see Sam preparing to get in to the BMW. I walk up to him and ask him, "Hey, would you like to try and keep pace with me while we drive back...?" "Are you crazy... at this hour?" he asks me, I just nod my head and provoke him a little by saying "Oh c'mon, don't tell me you can't do it... I need to do a speed check on my car anyway, so why not try... I know you can keep up with me...let's do it, for my sake." He agrees but in the back of my mind I know Sam cannot beat me because the BMW speed gets locked at 233 kilometres per hour but the Ferrari has a higher speed limit.

I get in to the Ferrari with Wang fast asleep in the passenger seat. I fasten the seat belt onto him and try fastening up my seat belt as well but it doesn't lock... oh c'mon... I try again and it still does not lock. Then, I realise that Wang's left hand is resting on the buckle and this is causing the problem. "Oh c'mon Wang, you want me to be riding without the seat belt fastened and risk my life eh?" I ask him but he is still asleep and cannot hear me. I just move his hand away and clamp the seatbelt in place. Sam is waiting for me and his engine is running. Now, my only thought is to start racing and clock the speed. I then try starting the car but am not able to... oh my God, not again... what's happening? I calm myself, try again and this time, the sound of the 2B exhaust is music to my ears.

I give the thumbs up sign to Sam and putting my left hand out of the window, begin the countdown by closing my fingers one by one - five... four... three... two... one and yippee... we're off! I keep an eye on the clock to see how much time I take to go from 0 to 100... it's 4.4 seconds, just one micro second more than the time claimed by the company. I notice that Sam is right behind me. There's very little traffic on the road and so I decide to step it up and as I do so, remember the Laguna Seca racing event I had been to and imagine myself to be on a race track racing with some of the world's best champion racers... and I zoom ahead!

I touch 190... vroom... 210 and then 225, and notice that Sam has gone out of sight and obviously, is way behind... it is sheer thrill and excitement, and I have never experienced anything like this before...it feels like this is a race that's more between man and machine. I try to stay focussed on the road ahead... I want to do more... and, just as I touch 240, I see the Interstate 280 highway I am driving on sloping down a little towards the left to connect to Highway 101... in seconds, as I reach the point still on 240 and swerve towards the left, oh... oh... oh my God! I suddenly find the car lifting off the ground and in the air...! In the flash of a second I remember how I handled a similar situation during a moving trip to Corpus Christi and spontaneously, turn the steering and hold it in this position.

The car surges ahead in the air for about six seconds and in those six seconds, I say a prayer, remember Mom and prepare myself for the worst. And then, the Ferrari hits the ground... spins around three times... the air bags come out... the car crashes in to a side barricade... again spins around two times... and finally comes to a halt. I look at Wang... he has hit his head against the windshield but is not bleeding...

I am conscious but unable to get myself out of the car... Sam who has been following me, reaches the spot, has a look at the car and approaches me with concern and worry writ large on his face... I try moving my arms and legs and as Sam and a few more people try to get me out of the car, I wonder if this is going to be the end of my chapter... and, I close my eyes... goodbye Mom... goodbye readers...